The
Wired
Church

Making Media Ministry

Len Wilson

D1383493

Abingdon Press
Nashville, Tennessee

THE WIRED CHURCH

Copyright © 1999 by Len Wilson

All rights reserved.

This book is printed on recycled, acid-free paper.

Library of Congress Cataloging-in-Publication Data on file

Wilson, Len, 1970–
    The wired church : making media ministry / Len Wilson.
       p. cm.
    ISBN 0-687-06915-7 (alk. paper)
       1. Public worship—Audio-visual aids.   2. Church work—Audio
-visual aids.   I. Title.
    BV288.W55   1999
     254′.3—dc21
                                         99-28169
                                            CIP

4th Printing
MANUFACTURED IN THE UNITED STATES OF AMERICA

This edition of *The Wired Church* is packaged with a CD-ROM that will significantly improve your grasp of the content in this book. The three interactive parts of the CD include:

Tutorials:
A breakdown of the creative process in creating images for projection during worship services. The tutorial shows the layers of a graphic, offers design tips, and demonstrates the top ten looks desired for a presentation graphic.

Technical:
A tour of the four primary options for configuring a worship space with screens, hardware, lighting, and sound.

Samples:
A portfolio of animations, videos, and graphics that can be used in worship presentation.

How to View the CD-ROM

QuarkImmedia Viewer is a stand-alone application that allows anyone to view and interact with QuarkImmedia projects. The QuarkImmedia Viewer is distributed royalty-free.

QuarkImmedia Viewer 1.5 is available for Windows, Macintosh, and Power Macintosh. The Windows version is compatible with Windows 95 and 98. Version 1.5 on the CD-ROM will be installed to your hard-drive. The CD-ROM, however, is hundreds of megabytes, containing many movies, and will be run from your CD-ROM player. You will need a sound card with speakers to fully appreciate the sounds and the graphics. Minimum requirements are a 486 processor and 8MB of RAM with 256 colors for the monitor. We have obtained best viewing results with at least a Pentium 166mghz and 32 MB of RAM, and at least an 8x CD-ROM.

Installation

Windows installation:
To install QuarkImmedia Viewer on your hard-drive, from the Start Menu (Windows 95 or 98), select RUN, X:\install.exe, where X is the letter of your CD-ROM drive. Close all open applications and follow the screen directions. When the viewer is installed, launch it from the program group or desktop. You may open the CD-ROM, by selecting FILE\Open X\wired.imd. See the file Read_1st.wri for further

information.

Macintosh installation:

Copy the Quarkimmedia Viewer file to the hard drive of your computer. (You can run Quarkimmedia Viewer directly from the CD, but performance may improve if you run it from your hard drive.) Double click the file Wired on the CD to play.

QuickTime installation:

To install the 32-bit version of QuickTime 3.0 from the CD-ROM:

• Open My Computer (Windows 95 or 98).
• Double-click on your CD-ROM drive.
• Double-click on the QUICKTIME3.O.EXE file or icon and follow the installation instructions for QuickTime 3.0.
• Double-click on the Wired.imd file or icon and enjoy!

To find the Wired.imd file:

• Open My Computer (Windows 95 or 98)
• Double click on your CD-ROM Drive
• Double click on the Wired.imd file or icon and enjoy

To receive technical support on installation of the CD-ROM, call Abingdon Software technical support at 1-615-749-6777 (hours: 8:30 a.m. to 4 p.m. CST, Monday through Friday).

Please visit your local bookstore for further copies of this work, or regarding sales matters, including returns. You may also order additional copies of this work at www.cokesbury.com.

This book is the perfect tool! It provides the church a clear rationale for presenting the gospel in today's terms, and it offers a step-by-step process for setting it up.

Virginia Greer, worship coordinator,
Asbury United Methodist Church, Corpus Christi, Texas

This book is a "must have" resource for anyone seeking to implement multisensory worship. It covers the technical methods and the foundational purposes necessary to carry us forward into the next century and beyond.

Andre Daley, Lead Pastor, CentrePoint,
Grand Rapids, Michigan

Hundreds of funerals are held daily for people who rejoiced in the arrival of color photographic slides. Their grandchildren prefer videotapes. If you are preaching to the grandparents, use a slide projector. If you want to communicate with their children and grandchildren, read this book.

How do you proclaim the gospel of Jesus Christ? During the past two millennia we have passed through four stages: 1) the spoken word, 2) the printed word, 3) the arts, and 4) good deeds. We are now in the fifth stage; electronic media. The Wired Church explains both the why and the how for any church leader that is ready to embrace the media reformation.

Lyle E. Schaller,
author of The Church Consultant, on CD-ROM

Wow! You don't read The Wired Church. You experience it. I went from macro to micro and back again & then wide angle to visualize the whole environment of Gospel and modern culture. Then I was plummeted into the heart of the spiritual leader of the media team, picturing Kairos moments through the intelligent eyes of a media-savvy missionary of Jesus Christ. Not only does the book tell you how to do it and who should do it, but how to phase it in, and why even the small church should start now. You really can start anywhere in the book. The best advice I can give a congregation is to just start somewhere immediately with *The Wired Church*!

Thomas Bandy,
author of Kicking Habits, and Growing Spiritual Redwoods

ACKNOWLEDGMENTS

I thank God for many people who have furthered my passion for media in renewing the church.

As a youth, my father Wayne Wilson encouraged me by nurturing the discipline of daily writing. His living words have continued to grow, giving me the freedom to believe that I can do anything, such as write a book.

The nearby community of United Theological Seminary has been instrumental in helping me refine my call, including Dennis Benson, Ken Bedell, Tom Boomershine, Larry Ramey, and Newell Wert. Trustee Charles Cappleman graciously gave of himself during my internship at CBS Hollywood.

I'm thankful to lead pastor Mike Slaughter and the hothouse he has created at Ginghamsburg Church for "birthing miracles." The worship design team, in particular Debra Welder, Kim Miller, Jason Moore, and Mike Lyons, make the wired church possible: no media minister can attempt this ministry alone.

My partner in ministry, Jason Moore, has made this project much better than it would have been through his commitment to excellence in his work on the CD-ROM, cover art, and icons. The media ministry team at Ginghamsburg has done the tedious work of producing weekly worship for years. These incredible, faithful servants include Connie Pack, Wendell Quinton, Alan Miles, Vicki Sybenga, David Brown, Mark Fish, Steve Gallimore and countless others.

I'm also thankful to my wife Shar, who has propped me up emotionally and spiritually over the course of the past year.

Never, never attempt to build a wired church alone.

>‹‹●››‹

Contents

Preface

Is Your Church Culture-Compatible?

How does this sound to you: "If you would speak with me, you must first learn my language"?

Voltaire, the great philosopher of the Enlightenment, spoke these words to those who would converse with him about the mysteries of life. He would deign to talk with you, but only if you smartened up to his level. Voltaire refused to dumb down.

Apple Computer also spoke these words to the world of its day. Its Macintosh had the best interface. It had the best graphics. It led the desktop publishing revolution. It was more "user-friendly" out of the box. But because it refused to be "compatible" with other computer companies, because they refused to "dumb down" their operating system, Mac lost out to Big Blue, which encouraged a variety of "IBM-compatibles."

Coming from a philosopher, or coming from a computer company, these words sound arrogant, proud, and elitist. But the Church speaks these same words to the culture every Sunday—and every other day of the week, for that matter. But unlike Voltaire and Apple, the Church's language is not a current one but an outmoded print language that is out of touch with how most people today live and move and have their being.

Besides, what if God had refused to "dumb down"? The Church wouldn't be here. The essence of the Incarnation is God's willingness to employ *kenosis* (emptying) toward the end of *plerosis* (filling). God dumbed down that we might be smartened up.

Len Wilson's book is designed as a companion piece to Mike Slaughter's key resource *Out on the Edge* (1998). But Wilson's work stands on its own as an indispensable toolbox for ministry in postmodern culture. The advent of electronic technology creates a new space, a whole new environment for worship, education, and every feature of the Church. You think the invention of farming was momentous? You think the invention of the printing press was momentous? Every day brings another breakthrough wrought by the microprocessor.

For any church to fail to pay attention to these revolutions is to go under. "If Pope Gregory said that icons were the Bible for the illiterate," Wilson writes, "then the screen is the Bible for the post-literate." Imagine doing ministry in the modern world and boasting, "I don't read." Imagine doing ministry in the postmodern world and boasting, "I don't do computers." Wilson quotes Neil Postman's *Amusing Ourselves to Death* a couple of times. He's kinder than I am. For a professor of communications like Postman to repudiate the chief medium of communications in our culture (the screen) would be like a professor of literature, such as Harold Bloom, to repudiate books.

No longer is print the metaphor of choice; it's now the Web. Media literacy or what I call "graphicacy" involves more than slapping print up on a screen. One of my favorite portions of this book is Wilson's disavowal of what he calls the "AV mentality," or in another place, "the shoving of rounded mouths into square screens." In the "AV mentality" the "use of electronic media is an afterthought, an add-on, or something less than an integral ingredient in worship and church life. An AV mentality is one in which the new communication form's primary use is to communicate themes and messages still centrally located, developed, and implemented within old communication forms such as mass print culture. . . . Video, audio, and graphics become merely support pieces for the primary communication tool of text." Wilson makes it clear that the transition from modern to post-modern is the transition from linear to nonlinear modes of thought. To do ministry in the modern world, the watchword was Get Linear. To do ministry in the post-modern world, the watchword is Get Looped.

Why are religious leaders having such problems making the transition from literacy to graphicacy, from linear to looped, from writing sermons to creating experiences? Wilson gives us a hint: it means "giving up control of the most powerful weapon of a pastor/leader's leadership, the pulpit." The sermon is still a viable communication form. "The success of the stand-up comedian verifies that," Wilson writes. But "just as the sermon mutated from a storytelling to an exegetical experience in the mass print era, it must mutate again, along with other elements of the Christian experience, to a tool that speaks to this new electronic culture."

Wilson's book helps us see the contours of that mutation as every "celebrant" becomes an artist and worship becomes an art form. Robert Shaw, the greatest choral conductor of the previous century (the twentieth century actually dates from 1914 to 1989), suggested at his Nashville, Tennessee, workshop a few years ago that just as the Church saved the arts in the medieval world, it may be the arts that save the Church in the new world that is dawning. Whether Shaw had in mind the high, folk, or pop arts is less relevant than that worship is being transformed and "saved" by the celebration arts.

There is much more I wish Wilson had said in print that he has said at seminars in person. You can expect to hear and see a lot more from this emerging leader. For example, one of the greatest hoaxes perpetrated on the contemporary mind is that electronic culture creates passive people. Immediately prior to writing this preface I read an article in which Web-based learning was panned and banned because we allegedly live in a world where "people mistake the virtual experience for the real." According to this author, "Kids are just as likely to sit in front of their computers and 'play' baseball as go outside and pitch and bat." Exactly the opposite is the case. When you surf the Net you want to surf Big Sur more. Electronic culture creates *interactive*, not passive people.

But there is more than enough here to show that the theory and practice of ministry are being transformed by new communications technology. For all ministers—and not just Ministers of Sound, Ministers of Light, Ministers of Videography, Ministers of the Celebration Arts—this book is a great place to start the transformation.

Leonard Sweet,
Dean of The Theological School and Vice President,
Drew University
Madison, New Jersey

Introduction

The purpose of this book:

- To prepare the leader of media ministry with the basic knowledge and skills required for a church that communicates in ways that new generations understand.
- To empower a culture that allows media teams to spring up where there are currently none.
- To show that creating eye-popping media is not rocket science.
- To demonstrate that the budget doesn't need to equal that of NASA.

What is not covered in this book:

- You will not find many specific brand names and product reviews of electronic media hardware and software. The landscape of the media industry changes too rapidly to cover these details with any certainty. However, there are many references to types of equipment, and suggested resources for more information.
- You will not encounter technical information regarding sound amplification. Sound ministry falls under the umbrella of electronic media, but in practice is a separate entity, with its own levels of expertise and interpretation.

Helpful icons:

Funding Fodder. Good ammunition for convincing your budget committee(s) that media ministry is essential, and not just cool stuff for youth and males who like electronic toys.

Dictionary. A funny new word? Here's what the jargon means.

Media 101. Basic theory so you can pass out of the Introduction to Electronic Media class.

Nuggets. Bits of wisdom to make you a better media guru.

 On the CD. Your CD-ROM gives multiple samples, examples, and techniques. Check it out. It's free with the book purchase!

 Interactive. Yes, you do want to try this at home.

The book contains four parts,

1. Developing a mission for media. Before your media ministry can have a lasting impact within the kingdom of God, you must identify a purpose. These basic guidelines will also help you gain approval when advocating change within a church culture.

2. Designing eye-popping media. You'll discover what type of electronic media is merely wallpaper, and what type communicates the Gospel in fresh, lucid ways. On top of that, you'll see basic guidelines for implementing your ideas.

3. Building a championship team. An electronic media studio in your church requires a number of volunteer specialists. This section will give you basic guidance on recruiting and training a team.

4. Buying the tools. The technical aspects of a media ministry are not like building a skyscraper. You will find a few basic things about equipment that will get you started. And you will find a number of suggested resources for discovering more information about media tools.

Part One:
Developing a Mission for Media

The Mission of the Church

Speak the Gospel in the language of the culture.

At a workshop on media in congregational ministry, a listener questioned me about the specific costs involved in producing high-quality media. I outlined a cost comparison between funding media ministry and funding more established communication forms, such as the newsletters and organs. When I mentioned the organ, a man in the back of the room groaned and interrupted with the exclamation that his church had spent $1.3 million for a new organ. He was mortified because he realized that his church had spent so much money ensuring continued success at speaking to a small faction of his church culture through an organ. Now, his church is impoverished when it comes time to speak to the culture through electronic media.

A mismatched mission can harm and even destroy congregational attempts to change and grow. A church is likely to fail by buying a van full of equipment and by throwing "stuff" on the screen, without any concept of what it is doing. An effective mission statement is crucial for the beginning of a viable media ministry, for several reasons:

- A written mission statement keeps members of the ministry focused.

- Literally, the media minister or church leader must cast the big picture by getting a clear understanding of the audience before powering up the tools.

- A mission statement will lead to judicious spending of limited funds, support of key congregational leaders, and an understanding of what electronic media look like and are intended to do.

The following chapter will help you formulate your mission statement for media ministry.

What is electronic media?

Media is plural for *medium,* which is an agent for transmitting messages between senders and receivers. Messages can be anything from "I love you" to the civil warning siren that goes off in rural towns twice a month. Electronic media are a means to send a message or set of messages to individuals or groups of people in which electronic forms of technology are utilized. Traditionally the electronic forms have consisted of a group of mass communication tools such as radio, film, television, CD-ROMs, and the Internet.

mass communication: masses of people receive the same sent message

The term *media* has come to signify any mass form of communication, and even the industry that creates its messages. Further, electronic media refers to this set of communication tools as a singular grouping, particularly in reference to the profound cultural changes they have brought about in the twentieth century.

As distinct from the detached analysis and criticism, typical of pre-twentieth-century book reading and research, electronic media is characteristically narrative in form, which means that it is adept at telling stories. This narrative purpose is in direct contrast to mass print culture, the culture of book reading and research that preceded electronic media.[1] Its strength in storytelling is due to powerful engagement of the senses on multiple levels through visual and aural imagery.

Stocking the Media Store

The production and distribution of messages are equally important in electronic media. Distribution in electronic culture is similar to shelf space at a grocery superstore. There are limited time and space in broadcasting for messages. Big industrial conglomerates have taken up most of the prime shelf space. (In the broadcast world, religion is the imported garbanzos next to the public access pig's feet.) Instead of fighting for space, however, local church media ministers have the opportunity of manufacturing their own messages and distributing them in their own environment, which allows for a more direct market that circumvents the broadcast superstore. The caution, as you will see, is that while the "products" may bring in an extra bit of business because of their convenience, they can't taste like gruel and expect to attract repeat visitors.

Electronic communication forms are becoming more viable in small group and individual communication settings, as computer technology becomes assimilated in Western culture. Business environments use graphics and video for meetings involving no more than ten persons; friends across the globe send e-mail and even talk to one another via Internet chat rooms. This increase corresponds to a democratic change affecting electronic media, from passivity to interactivity. The definition of electronic media, then, will continue to evolve as the technological components mature and as technologies communicate to smaller settings and in more dynamic ways.

Electronic media may be referred to as simply "media." A media ministry, then, uses video, audio, graphics, text, and other technology applications to communicate the Gospel message.

What are the nature and purpose of electronic media in church life?

Media ministry is so broad that it may take on many different forms. This book will help you understand these distinctions and their impact on ministry decisions.

Universities construct fields of discipline in a helpful way. At a large university a student has the option to pursue media through fine arts (a theater or literature major, for example), through traditional, mass forms such as radio and television (mass communication major), through orality (speech major), through tactile forms (art majors), through written forms (English or journalism majors) or through computer technology (information systems major). Each is a valid media form. Each addresses specific media as communication tools. Some of the ways, then, to understand the potential role of media may be characterized into the following four categories:

Four Ways to Understand Media in Ministry

1. Media as the arts

One understanding of media is defined as a means to (re)create the impact and experience of fine art. The fine arts have been traditionally thought of as stage, dance, sculpture, literature, painting, poetry, (what is now known as) classical music, film, and so on. Prior to the twentieth century the purpose of the arts for the Church was to re-create the divine through representations of beauty and truth. The theological basis for the arts is largely one that views God as the manifestation of all that is good, beautiful, and true. Applied to the Gospel, the arts aim to create a response in which the receiver perceives God through interpretations that engage the soul and the spirit.

Prior to the electronic age, fine arts set the cultural standard. After its inception as a state religion under Constantine in the fourth century, Christianity became the keeper of fine art and through it the standard-bearer for cultural norms. Pope Gregory made the announcement at the dawn of the seventh century that the arts were the primary means to disciple the uneducated and "unchurched," although he didn't use that word. He called the arts, "the Bible for the illiterate." The cultural Renaissance of the fifteenth and sixteenth centuries was fueled by the arts, and was to a degree subsidized by the Church, particularly in the areas of music and sculpture. Persons of all socio-economic backgrounds partook of the arts.

During the twentieth century, however, there has been a transition in Western culture away from the fine arts as the cultural pacesetter. Fine arts have become increasingly abstract, ambiguous, and driven by an abandonment of the notion of objective truth. The worldview of artists have become increasingly relativistic, and abandoning the Judeo-Christian value system of the religious and cultural benefactors. Simultaneously, electronic media permeated society, turning the populace to more common creative expressions. *Time* magazine, in a commemorative issue on the top artists and entertainers of the twentieth century, said, "Literature, the theater, classical music [have] lost the authority to set the cultural agenda. Today, the influence, the action, the buzz is all pop."[2] Pop art has replaced fine art.

Some art advocates in the Church speak of the need to "reclaim" the arts for the kingdom of God. This desire is commendable if art is once again an agent of the Gospel, sponsored by and created with the aid of the Church. What will not happen, however, at least in our lifetime, is a return of the fine arts to a former position of cultural authority, granted by sacred benefactors.

This shift is not to be mourned. Simply, the rules have changed. Pop art isn't the absence of art, as some fine art connoisseurs proclaim; its artistic beauty is in part found in its commonality. Creative expression in the electronic age has become democratic. God would have it that way. According to Genesis, God created all people in the image of the Creator. All people, thus, are creative. And with the birth of the new communication system of electronic media, many more people have the opportunity to express their innate creativity. And the consequences of that opportunity are proving explosive even within the communication arts. A fourteen-year-old in media ministry recently gave me her own homemade web site address. Software exists that enables children to create 3-D computer animation. The opportunities are incredible, and do not require the same degree of training as the fine arts demanded and regulated for entry into a guild.

Churches cannot change the mood of the mass culture.

The narrative theologian Frederick Beuchner says that the most powerful preaching for this age comes from the poets, playwrights, and novelists. He almost got it right, with amends for his print age bias. The most powerful preaching today is actually coming from the filmmakers, the standup comedians, and the producers.

Media is most effective as a communication system when it expresses art for the cultural majority. There are always subcultures present, which are to be addressed. But the primary, the global, reach of media is reflected through pop art expression. A return to fine arts is a "retro" move.

Our job, as messengers of the Gospel, is to speak in whatever language the culture is speaking. If Renaissance history is any barometer, we are about to ride a wave of explosive creativity, as this new medium grows out of pre-pubescent awkwardness and becomes fully assimilated into the lives of those with truth to speak, with media that forces the receivers out of their state of indifference.

2. Media as information

Manifestations of electronic media through the twentieth century have been primarily documentation, rather than interpretation. Radio, television, and now the Internet, the three largest electronic mediums, have been known more for the ability to disseminate information globally than for the ability to represent artistic truth. Most early radio professionals came from print culture disciplines such as the newspaper business; likewise, the heritage of television is radio. Television was touted as the first global medium, and its biggest victories came not through *M*A*S*H* and *Dallas*, both internationally popular programs, but in its ability to alert the world to breaking news stories as they happened. Vietnam was the first living room war. The world watched the British monarchy, in all of its pomp, get married. And even now, the Internet is the place for information, whether it is home run record statistics or news of political scandal.

Mass media of the twentieth century, as distinct from the artistic understanding of media, have been used primarily as information, a way to reach masses of people quickly. Many early attempts by the Church to use electronic media, mimicking the culture, approached it in this fashion. Mainline denominations constructed entire global news and information agencies for the purpose of processing and disseminating information. Rather than report bad news, or conflict, the Church would then report *good* news, and people's lives would be transformed.

We have learned again, however, that transmitting information is not the same thing as empowering transformation.

The twentieth century's move away from the notion of objective truth destroys the idea of media as information, however. Post-modern culture says, My truth is not the same as your truth, so who cares?

The use of media as an informational tool has been incomplete in transforming people into Christ's likeness. Readers may cognitively see or hear the power of Christ's love, but not be moved to act upon it themselves, because it doesn't engage their soul and spirit as art does.

Media as information, then, is the opposite of media as art.

Information isn't enough; presentation matters. Effective or excellent media for this age both engages the mind and the heart.

3. Media as mission or evangelism

The third use of media is for evangelism, for the purpose of drawing unchurched people into a faith community. This view recognizes that media is the central communication component of Western social life, and it sees media as a primary means in which to speak the culture's language. However, media in this use is for speaking outside the walls of the church community, and is not for the most part a central communication form within church life. Worship practices and discipleship forms within church life remain steeped in pre-electronic media culture. Media is only used for outreach or evangelism purposes, such as the occasional advertising campaign, out of a vague awareness that it is important at high times in the Christian year, based on the lectionary, to do a little promotion.

One problem with speaking the cultural language to the world but not to the church is that the product cannot match the advertisement. Any person will try something once. If the reality does not match the hype, then that person, the visitor, won't try again. An effective way to turn people away is to disguise messages by promoting one thing, only to actually present another message; that is, to promote media forms as a communication tool for spiritual truth but to provide hymnals and (not so fine) art upon arrival. The effect is similar to the promotional material that comes in the mail announcing a free cruise, but which can only be obtained, according to fine print restrictions, by purchasing a condominium. As advocates holler with zeal, Truth in Advertising!

It's not even that the messages aren't truthful. It's that the culture is media-savvy. It does little good to draw in visitors at a surface level when there is no system in place to continue speaking their language once they arrive.

Cultural participants now both understand the messages and interpret the medium that communicates them.

Contemporary effective messages must speak on multiple levels, using vertical communication, and not only horizontal communication. Simply put, the Church should not advertise in the marketplace until it is capable of delivering messages that are integrated with its internal communication matrix. On the Internet, many corporations have learned that they cannot handle an effective presence on the web without structurally supporting that through a pervasive Intranet, or an internal computer networking base.

To be in ministry means maintaining the constant tension between life in the Spirit and life on Earth.

It means seeing the secular culture as incorrect, but not evil, and the job of the Church to transform the outer culture to its rightful place as the kingdom of God. Salvation is not just for another time and place but for all people, now. Living in the gap of where we are in Christ and where the culture is without Christ, tense though that place may be, is where Christians are called to serve, because it is the only place in which the world can hear our messages. It does not mean living a dualistic life in which church culture is separate from secular culture.

4. Media as cultural language

The combination of the best of these three understandings of media, then, forms a fourth: media as cultural language. It should (*a*) mimic innovatation in pop cultural expression, (*b*) reach the mind and the soul, (*c*) through its expression of Christ and truth, draw people to God, and (*d*) mediate the presence of the Church in the world, for the sake of transforming the culture.

A few years ago media agencies latched onto the idea of a five-hundred-channel universe, which would be made possible through improved cable television bandwidth. It never materialized, though, because nobody in the news/entertainment/media matrix had enough to say. (In my local cable service, the programmers can't even fill seventy-six channels very well.)

bandwidth: **the size of the "pipe," or cable, through which data travels.**

A lack of content has never been an issue for the Gospel storyteller. The challenge of the Church is the opposite of the cultural challenge—to take our powerful, life-changing story, and present it in such a way that people understand.

Ezra did just that. After a long, dark night, things were coming together for the Israelites. Jerusalem's walls had been rebuilt, and the Temple was next. Ezra, who had been commissioned with the proclamation of the Law, finally got the opportunity to read it before the Israelites. Except, he had a problem. The cultural language from the making of the Law to the present day had changed, possibly to Aramaic, the language of the Israelites' Babylonian and Persian captors. So Ezra had Levite priests be an interpretive public address system, standing among the people as he read the Law. Nehemiah 8:8 says, "They read from the Book of the Law of God, translating it and giving the meaning so that the people could understand what was being read" (NIV). The consequence? Verse 9 says they wept for joy at the hearing of the Law, the Word of their God, because they finally understood. It had been spoken in their language.

The Gospel is powerful and attractive: any effective presentation of the Word of God has the potential to result in a life-changing experience for its hearers. For the media age, the challenge of ministers of any capacity is to speak with the same lucidity using our cultural language of media that the Levite priests did when they translated the Law for the people. If done well, the result will be changed lives and a renewed Church.

Our goal: to speak the Gospel in the language of the Culture.

The Shape of This Cultural Language

Storytelling

The messages that electronic media send may be classified as story, which is a colloquialism but also a reference to what Len Sweet calls the "ancient future," or a reinterpretation of the oral culture of early civilizations, in which the primary communication tool was the story.

Noted media theorist George Gerbner defines storytelling as the "shorthand" for the "magic" that is created out of our unique ability as a species to live in a world larger than our own immediate gratifications. It is the compilation of these stories that composes the seamless web of our culture.[3] In this understanding, stories are not fiction but the content or substance of the messages we send to one another individually and collectively, to edify and serve one another and the world around us.

In the mass print age, storytelling took a backseat to more formal symbiotic relationships. But the twentieth century has seen a resurgence of the metaphor as communication tool.

The concept of storytelling is apropos for electronic media, as its components lend themselves to narrative forms. Stories engage multiple senses. Visual and aural imagery add multiple dimensions of depth to the process of telling a story.

Personal stories of faith make for great media.

It is engaging and effective to hear a two-minute personal faith story through the medium of video, with an edited first-person retelling over an acoustic piano bed, and with shots of the teller's environment interspersed throughout.

This is much more compelling than the twenty minutes it would take the same person to awkwardly tell the story, using nothing but a microphone and a podium.

Jesus, a storyteller, would have been a communicator for the electronic media age: He used intimate distance, involving small groups with stories, parables, and images. Although fluent in the law and possibly in three languages (Hebrew, Greek, Aramaic) by the age of twelve, Jesus did not communicate in the methodology of the Temple thinkers, but instead he chose to speak to the populace in a language that they could understand. Obviously, his message was heard. It is the reception of the story that is critical.

Excellence

How many people do you know who watch public access television on a regular basis? Established by Congress and intended to provide cultural dialogue in an age of broadcast hegemony, public access instead became the forum of video geeks everywhere, and their messages have indeed been varied, but almost always unclear and poorly produced.

hegemony: when all the messages being injected into the culture are saying the same thing

Public access broadcast as an inexpensive distribution route for local church media can be a dangerous option, as the church often becomes guilty by association. My local cable public access channel airs the weekly show, "Devil-line" right after one of their broadcasted church services. The result of a channel of shocking and poorly produced media is that no one watches, and the moral is that whatever Christian media has to say, it's got to be said well.[4]

It has been said that much of the media industry is operating within a vacuum of values. One reason is that the Church has been unwilling to make the sacrifices necessary to speak the language of the culture fluently, or with excellence. Our halfhearted messages come out under our breath, slurred and monotone.

I met a number of producers in Hollywood who have given up on the idea of integrating their faith into their passion for the electronic media age. One was a man who was the associate producer of a long-running daytime game show. He and a number of other professionals with active faith life had all chosen to live and work in Southern California, in the attempt to have positive influence on the culture at large from within the secular entertainment industry. This leader understood the value of excellence, and during our conversation he specifically pointed out recent attempts at translating the Gospel into the cultural language such as the film *The Judas Project* as a reason why he was no longer attempting to integrate his faith and vocation. To him, *The Judas Project* was a poorly done work that did not interpret the Gospel in an attractive visual way. Saying it right mattered so much to him that he would rather produce a game show with money prizes, and with a budget, than the Gospel story without a budget.

To me, he seemed right about the importance of excellence, but it was frustrating that he had no concept or model of how to tell the Gospel story effectively, outside of the entertainment business. His concept mimicks the general approach to media ministry within the Christian community, which merely adds a Judeo-Christian veneer to the porous moral mire found in the messages of the entertainment industry.

Our calling is to transform the culture.[5]

The world will always be as a whole lost without the transforming power of Jesus Christ. Trying to change the entire culture, by a return to the pseudo-Christian days of *Ozzie and Harriet,* will only be met with frustration and failure. The way to transform the culture is through individuals and the work of the congregation. Tip O'Neill, the late Speaker of the House, coined the political phrase, "Think Global, Act Local." True, lasting change occurs one small step at a time. For us this means telling electronic media stories in local church contexts for the purpose of evangelism, edification, discipleship, and transformation.

Excellence requires us to tell these stories with lucidity. The opposite of clear communication is "noise," another apropos term for electronic media. Many recent Hollywood films, particularly during the summer seasons, avoid lucid storytelling, with an emphasis on special effects instead of plot development.

Clear communication occurs through a mostly invisible medium. Like the offensive linemen on a football team, a medium that does its job will elicit a score with the receiver, not a focus on its job of blocking out noise. The viewer should not say "What an effect!" but "What a story!" because the focus of the Gospel storyteller is to use media technology as tool, not toy.

In the late 1980s a company called NewTek revolutionized the video industry by introducing the first computer video editing machine, the Video Toaster. Suddenly, what had formerly cost a million dollars and a dedicated studio could now be accomplished with $10,000 in a small room with a desk. The product's strength, however, was also its weakness. With the democracy of video came a number of producers who mixed their video effects like so many poor verb tenses. The standard "sheep wipe" and thick drop shadowed text were seen in nearly every wedding and industrial video for almost a decade.

The lesson: There is a distinct difference between excellence and entertainment.

Be careful with your use of effects when learning to speak the media language. Nothing attracts more than a good story. Effects properly used will enhance the telling of the story, not detract.

Integration

The pervasiveness of the media age changes the way we conceptualize the use of media.

Having a big screen doesn't mean lowering it for a video clip or a graph of the church financial state, then raising it and returning to the good old days of doing church.

It means integrating imagery, video, and sound into the entire church experience, whether that is worship, education, administration, or outreach. "Raising the screen," or putting media in a compartment, means that the Church is not acknowledging its continued dependence on outdated forms of communication.

Many well-meaning inquirers say, "I want to do this to reach the youth." Youth groups are definitely one reason for the incorporation of electronic media, because youth and children speak this language innately. They've been raised from birth with its presence surrounding them, from Disney as the baby-sitter to CD-ROM interactive "edutainment" games, to Internet teen chat rooms, to standard broadcast television. They are completely media literate, understanding both how to send messages and how to receive them.

Don't merely use media as a gimmick to reach the youth.

But a media ministry is not only for youth or children. The members and visitors of your congregation, no matter what the age, watch thirty hours of TV per week or more. Electronic media is saturated throughout the culture. Television became a national phenomenon in the early 1950s, which means that the majority of kids born in the 1940s grew up with a screen. These youth are now about to turn sixty. TV is the staple of nursing homes. TV is the companion beside hospital beds. TV is the time killer at airport gates and terminals. Electronic media is everywhere and for people of all ages. So, as you implement and design electronic media for church life, don't just cater to the unchurched, or to certain age-groups or demographic niches. Make sure media is available to all, inside and out.

It is possible and even encouraged to alter design and layout of media to fit certain demographic groups. Follow the model established by broadcast entities. "Lifetime" network, aimed at women and an older audience, creates softer looks with its video and animation. Colors are usually light pastels, fonts are script, or serifed. ESPN, aimed at the adult male, creates bolder looks: lots of vibrant color schemes, with movement and animation, and much depth and the presence of lines in the design as well. MTV, with its edginess and seemingly broken down construction, fits younger viewers. Text cannot sit still, shifting about in place; colors are dark and light, connoting a flashiness and disruptive experience; the edges of the frame itself sometimes become visible, drawing attention in a deconstructed way to the very existence of the visual medium sending the messages. This style is the closest embodiment to Marshall McLuhan's adage that "the medium is the message," in that the message becomes the medium. That is a pointless message, if you ask me.

Integration means getting to the point in creative presentation where you're not aware of the screen anymore. Screen isn't a white elephant; media ministry means utilizing the screen as part of the overall matrix of church life.

Integrated media also means creating a blend of communication forms. Every new media system has shifted from a brief period of antagonism toward previous forms to a new, holistic understanding of how they fit together. A media-integrated church doesn't abandon the traditions of the Church, it reinterprets how that tradition speaks to its constituents at the place in which they live.

Turning the Gospel into Entertainment?

Critics of electronic media claim that these forms water down the power of the Gospel by turning it into consumer entertainment.[6] Here are three reasons why this is not true:

1. Media ministry is not vaudeville.

The first attempts at producing electronic media as ministry were practiced by the televangelists, who owe their legacy to characters such as Billy Sunday or Aimee Semple McPherson. These pioneers imitated vaudeville actors, who saw the nickelodeon and the radio as new ways in which to spread their message. Their entrepreneurial spirit laid the framework for the debate about "theology as entertainment," which has festered among Christian circles throughout the twentieth century. Denominations at the time insisted that radio networks provide airtime free of charge for the purpose of spreading the Gospel, as a public service. Networks complied, but of course it wasn't long before free time was allocated to Sunday morning. The cost was cheap for the networks and the least intelligent time for churches to speak the cultural language.

In spite of the opportunity to speak to a culture in its newly formed and fresh language, most established churches again managed to use communication systems as support structures for the status quo. It is analogous to the Roman Church's first use of the printing press, to enforce the "correct" Mass to outpost parishes who had adopted the Latin text to fit their milieu. Early media entrepreneurs assumed no such preferential treatment from a state or from a culture that was defined by its separation from the Church. Though Nielsen hadn't invented his rating system yet, their paid airtime was often in what we now call prime time, meaning that their messages were heard by masses of people.

As so often happens in the Church, however, over time medium and message became confused, and later mass media evangelists continued for the most part to model themselves after the vaudeville legacy of their predecessors. A legacy is not without merit; all good preachers model themselves after individuals who are successful at the art of public discourse. However, the methodology and mission for many televangelists are now passé. The challenge, then, is for presenters of new electronic media to reinvent what it means to speak the language of this culture.

Three Principles for Understanding the New Cultural Language

a) Recognize the dynamic context of electronic culture. Even as a "church junkie," theologian Tom Boomershine never stops to listen to televised sermons. He concludes that, "the sermon flunks the electronic culture viability test."[7] However, the failure of the sermon to be a viable form in electronic culture is just as much the fault of the Church's legacy of sermon preparation as it is due to the nature of the medium. Oral presenters are all over the tube, with the Comedy Channel a prime source. The sermon is not dead. It has merely mutated.

b) Let the mutation alter the way in which we communicate. If you preach a sermon over the airwaves, or across broadcast television, you shove a round peg into a square hole. It assumes that the best of one form of communication will work in another, completely different form. Preachers, like the dots on a screen, are "channels" of the same good news. But to put one form into another gives results much like the camera lens that sees a video monitor of itself: it loops into nothingness. To change the channel of preaching means that you shed the tactics of the vaudeville showperson and the tactics of the solitary iconoclast to discover how multiple forms of visual and aural communication will help to tell the Gospel story. Cultural literacy does not mean abandoning other forms of communication. Neil Postman, an electronic media naysayer, is correct when he asserts that "not everything is televisable."[8] Electronic media does not abandon previous mediums. Communicators now have an unprecedented plethora of storytelling options at their disposal.

c) Look to the best communicators of the day for "style" tips. Some of the best communicators are comedians and disc jockeys. These people combine oral discourse with imagery and sound. The valedictorians of comedy are the hosts of late-night television. It is no coincidence that these individuals restrain their opening monologues to a few minutes, then quickly utilize other media forms to keep the channel surfers at bay.

2. Questions on the nature and existence of electronic culture are irrelevant to the majority of North Americans.

By now we are in our third generation of television as the dominant communication form of the culture.[9]

High schoolers have grandparents who watched *The Honeymooners* as newlyweds. To deny electronic media as a feasible communication form now would put us among the separatist traditions that are well documented in Christian history, from the Essenes to the Amish.

The famous first Church debate found in Acts centers around the then "hot-button" issue of Gentiles, the Law, and life in Christ. Should certain laws be obeyed, or are non-Israelites exempt from the rituals that had character-ized God-followers for more than a millennium? As the Church became a Gentile-dominant Church, the question became moot. At some point, the "entertainment" ques-tion will also become moot, so long as the integrity of the Gospel is not lost in the translation. Fortunately, electronic media is created in teams, which in spiritual terms act as accountability groups.

3. Understand the distinctions between media and its messages.

The theological error of the early televangelists tends to overshadow their efforts, however crude, at translating the Gospel into a new, *mass* media. Their eagerness to expose so many people to the good news at once, outweighed concern they had about the impact of the media on the message.

There has been much debate over media pop guru Mar-shall McLuhen's idiom, "The medium is the message." Is the media the message? For McLuhen's time, in the 1960s, it was. Media was big news in the decade in which televi-sion played a major part in redefining the value system of a society.

The printing press was big news, too, when it came out. While Europeans were still getting used to the availability of the printed word, it may have been bigger news than the words that were being printed.

Eventually, the press was assimilated into daily life. So, now, too, has electronic media become assimilated into daily life.

This doesn't mean it's the only viable communication form. There are times and places in which particular medi-ums are best suited. To paraphrase Neil Postman, an e-mail condolence card, sent at your convenience, at the death of a friend's loved one doesn't compare to sacrificial face-to-face, interpersonal communication.

Similarly, some messages are best sent through the potential of electronic media. A printed description of the awesome first Temple, built by the people of Israel, with descriptions of measurable units, heighth and depth, and materials used in the construction, is not nearly as effective as a video virtual reality tour, in which the puny nature of our human size is contrasted against the height and breadth of the Temple's scope.

Media literacy is authentic when you use the appropriate medium for your message.

Fluency with the language of the culture is evidence of media literacy.

So, What Is a Media-Literate Church?

The training required for electronic media is similar to expectations for expertise in any other communication tool.

Have you ever wondered why some sermons are so ineffective and unmemorable?

Simply put, the audience has had no intrinsic training in how to listen. The pace needed for effective listening is more than most people are willing to give. With the combination of weak listening skills and ineffective preaching skills, the back door to the Church is wide open.

Every new communication system, as with any new language, must be taught. It's a form of literacy. A new language is easiest to learn and retain when it occurs in the majority culture. Electronic media is indigenous because most people have heard the tongue since the day they were born.

It's not a skill but a fundamental form.

A media-literate person is no longer aware of media as a language or means of communication. It is a fundamental cognitive system of communication. In fact, resistance to media ministry usually arises out of ignorance of media as a formational system.

When I finished formal education I joined many unemployed and underemployed college graduates with degrees in communication and media, probably because media was still institutionally a skill. Most universities taught it only as a means of understanding sociological impact. "True" instruction still occurred at the literate level. But as the print culture fades, its purveyors are discovering what everyone else already knew: that media is no longer a profession; it is an entire system of communication. Electronic forms coexist at the developmental stage with printed forms of literacy. Now, a four-year-old child can edit a video.

Fluency means saying new things, too.

The fluent church leader is not just a producer of worship. We are producers of culture by observing and editing the trends of the culture at large. In fact, it is these very trends that often give inspiration that may be adapted to our own contexts.

There's really nothing new. Creativity is simply hiding your sources.

However, even while looking to the culture for nuances of this visual language, do not:

• Let the meaning within the media programming determine the meaning within your messages;
• Become bound to the very forms that inspire you.

Artists set the cultural agenda as much as they imitate it. Most great artists may be classified as either innovators or perfecters. Handel the innovator, Mozart the perfecter. Miles the innovator, Wynton the perfecter. As the filmmaker Steven Spielberg once said in an interview:

> We define our times as we live them. Every time a studio plays it safe and says this isn't the right time for a western, some western comes out and succeeds. Who would have thought a costume drama, a love story aboard a boat that sinks, was going to move anybody? The times define themselves as we move through time. The pundits that start to predict what's right and wrong, what's good timing or bad timing, I used to listen to that, and recently I just don't. I just sort of shoot in the dark.[10]

A media-literate producer is capable of speaking the language with fluency and saying something in a new way. A Gospel storyteller who can achieve this will empower a human being beyond any message that the world may have to state.

---

[1] Mass print is one of many macro-systems that have categorized the communication styles of civilization throughout history. Communication typologies, or means of categorizing these systems, have been well documented, most recently in *Out on the Edge: A Wake-Up Call for Church Leaders on the Edge of the Media Reformation* (Abingdon Press, 1997), pp. 58-63.

[2] "Right Before Our Eyes," Christopher Porterfield, *Time* magazine, June 6, 1998, p. 69.

[3] "Epilogue: Advancing on the Path of Righteousness (Maybe)," George Gerbner, *Cultivation Analysis: New Directions in Media Effects Research*, N. Signorielli and M. Morgan, eds. (Unpublished), p. 250.

[4] The cynical version of this is Blues Traveler's top-ten song "Hook," which suggests that the messages don't matter as long as the metaphor sticks.

[5] To understand what this means and examine some other categories for understanding the Christian role in the culture, read *Christ and Culture*, by H. Richard Neibuhr. Then read *Resident Aliens* by Stanley Hauerwas and William Willimon (Abingdon Press, 1989), which is an important challenge to Neibuhr's social agenda. This is required reading for anyone trying to integrate cultural language into church life.

[6] A common assertion from critical books such as Neil Postman's *Amusing Ourselves to Death* and Gregor Goethal's' *The Electronic Golden Calf: Images, Religion and the Making of Money*, which are both products of highly literate practitioners who sense obsolescence.

[7] "The Polish Cavalry and Christianity in Electronic Culture," Boomershine, Tom. *United Seminary Journal of Theology*, 1996, p. 4.

[8] Postman, Neil, *Amusing Ourselves to Death: Public Discourse in the Age of Show Business* (Penguin Books, 1985), p. 118.

[9] It may be the last generation, though, as the passive medium of television gives way to the cultural forums and channels of the Internet.

[10] Steven Spielberg, *Mr. Showbiz* interview, June 28, 1998, www.mrshowbiz.com.

Part Two:
Designing Eye-Popping Media

With many elements involved in putting together media for a live event such as worship, how does it all come together? Let's begin at the end with the big picture, and then move into deeper explanation of terms and functions. The following four steps suggest a sample outline for one week in the life of a media ministry. At some point there can be too many cooks stirring a pot, but for nearly any church, the more people with specific gifts that are involved, the higher the quality of the worship experience.

These steps show what might happen in a mature environment as you gain experience. If you are just starting, the basic steps remain, but with fewer complex activities.

Step 1 : Brainstorming process

- Identify the one great idea or theme for the weekend and the metaphor to illustrate it.
- Begin thinking about how to visually represent the chosen theme and metaphor for the weekend.
- Identify possible pre-produced video clips.
- Coordinate talent and any production personnel, a location (if necessary), and all the equipment.
- Make a storyboard for specific shots that will be needed and plan graphics for the video.
- Sketch rough drawings of what the worship image might be.

Step 2: Acquire elements

- Shoot video(s) on location.
- Rent film(s) for any movie clips.
- Finalize sketch of primary worship graphic.
- Log/digitize video clips from a shoot.
- Choose a music bed for the video.
- View rented films.

Step 3: Editing

- Edit video.
- Meet with the preacher to review graphics.
- Identify a few (interpretive) illustrations.
- Coordinate the collection of any needed graphic elements.
- Create a technical script based on the sermon notes, outlining graphics in their respective locations.
- Shoot/scan/digitize/create graphic elements.
- Key in song lyrics and scripture text.
- Compose the graphic illustrations.

Step 4: More editing and rehearsal

- Analyze the sermon again, to finalize graphic needs for the weekend of worship.
- Produce eleventh-hour changes.
- Coordinate the presentation of all the media elements in the live setting.
- Run through key points at least twice.

Worship begins!

Beyond the AV Mentality

As a Christian who watches television, I find that channel surfing can be a bittersweet experience. On my local cable system, there is a cluster of channels in the 20–30 range. These qualify as the "spiritual" channels, such as EWTN (the Catholic network), Odyssey (the Protestant network), Z-TV (Christian music videos), Trinity Broadcasting Network ("televangelism"), PAX-TV ("family" programming), and even local churches who air their worship services. In spite of an active personal faith, as I pass by these channels, almost without fail, I have no desire to stop and watch the programming. As far as I can tell, by doing some unscientific polling among other Christians, I am in the majority. It is certainly true that these networks receive low Nielsen ratings, even when compared to other niched networks such as Home and Garden TV and the Animal Planet. Based on the occasional times I do stop and watch, I don't think for the most part it is because of poor production values or lack of meaningful content. Their listings are even in the guides published in our local newspaper.

The reason, perhaps, is that most religious television does a poor job of interpreting the Gospel to an electronic culture. Church television comes across as "church-y" television, an object of parody regardless of what kind of faith the viewer has. Much of the programming on these channels still consists of live worship experiences, theological discussions, and performances by musical groups, which are each forms appropriate to a faithful life but not necessarily fitting in the electronic medium of television. The other most common form, the narrative or drama, requires a regular audience that is rare in the world of niche-market cable TV.

For years social critics have mocked the efforts of church leaders in media, using derisive terms such as "electronic church" to connote morally bankrupt shysters who front religion for financial gain. While a few bad apples continue to spoil the pot, it remains that the forms that church television uses look different from the rest of television. Regardless of programming decisions to target church or unchurched audiences, if Christian programming fails to reach Christians, it is probably not going to reach the public.

This lack of interpretation in electronic media, whether in broadcast or within a local church, is what I call the "AV mentality." The AV mentality is the use of electronic media as an afterthought, an add-on, a value to be added, or something less than an intrinsic ingredient in worship and church life. An AV mentality is one in which the new communication form's primary use is to communicate themes and messages still centrally located, developed, and implemented within old communication forms such as mass print culture. The AV mentality is interested more in documentation than interpretation. Video, audio, and graphics become merely support pieces for the primary communication tool of text.

Media at its most shallow level is merely illustrative or "enhancement." But at a transformational level, media is interpretive, or capable of saying things not possible to say in other forms. Everyone who watches movies understands the difference when they see it. It is the difference between an AA video on alcoholism and Robert Duvall's performance as an alcoholic who goes on the wagon in *Tender Mercies*. It is the difference between *Shadowlands*, C. S. Lewis's December discovery of relational love as a reflection of God, and my favorite example of how not to reach youth, *SuperChristian*. As noted, literacy at the level of consumption is fairly saturated in this, our third adult generation of electronic media cultural dominance. But understanding the difference at a conceptual level, which is necessary to the development and implementation of effective electronic media ideas, means utilizing a combination of biblical exegesis and storytelling. It means thinking visually. It means the use of metaphors.

Electronic media are merely tools, no different from any other tool used to communicate the Gospel throughout history, whether that is the scroll, the podium, the pencil, the mimeograph machine, or the hot-metal press. Accepting this is the key to fully separating media from its messages. For example, a cross mounted in a sanctuary is not an image to be worshiped. Versions of the cross, whether they are wooden or glass or metal, are like stained glass and other media, representative forms for truth as contained in the Scriptures. Although they may be effective communication forms for worship and church life, they are no more than the best media from an earlier age, still finding function in our current synthesis. Churches that must have the cross in the sanctuary may not realize that they are focusing on a representation, however important, of the resurrected Christ, and not on Jesus himself. This sacralization of an icon, however central to faith, draws inevitable comparisons to the Roman church's veneration of icons prior to the Reformation. A cross, hung in a sanctuary, is not *the* cross from Golgotha, and Jesus is not still hung on it.

The screen is the stained glass, and the cross, for the electronic media age, except now we have the privilege of working in a dynamic rather than a static form. The screen is the ever-changing canvas, constantly transposing new imagery before us. If Pope Gregory persuaded us that icons were the Bible for the illiterate, then the screen is the Bible for the post-literate.

Understandably, church leaders often have a hard time with this transition. For this there are at least two reasons. First, they have been trained differently. Seminaries are bastions of the mass print culture of books and analysis. Most preaching classes, where communication techniques are taught, at our theological seminaries are exercises in exegesis and analysis, that often bypass a narrative focus in electronic storytelling and cultural literacy. Most pastors and church leaders who have been seminary trained, no matter what their experience and exposure to electronic media culture, must decide after graduation whether to make the radical shift to the presence and use of electronic media.

A typical transition for a pastor, preacher, or church leader into electronic media initially means continuing to compose sermons without brainstorming groups or electronic media input, then finally tacking on AV support to a completed message. Over time, a leader's understanding gradually molts to composing central themes and structural points and then using media to communicate these points, to finally utilizing visual concepts in the conceptual stage of planning. Unfortunately, many leaders never get beyond the first step because it means sharing responsibility of this creative process with others. It means forming creative teams. This is the second reason, giving up control of the most powerful icon of a pastor's leadership, the pulpit.

The problem is compounded in the Protestant tradition because the sermon is the core element of the worship experience. But, contrary to what some have suggested, interpreting the Gospel to our culture does not mean an abandonment of the sermon as a viable form. And the formation of this new wineskin will occur through replication and adaptation of methodologies already in place in current visual industries and in the arts.

Rather as the sermon mutated from a storytelling to an exegetical experience in the mass print era, it must mutate again, along with other elements of the Christian experience, into a form that speaks to this electronic culture.

Fortunately for the Church, broadcast television is in the pre-pubescent stage of electronic media as a communication system. Its reputation as an isolated, isolating experience fails to take into account the metamorphosis that is occurring as the system matures over hundreds of years into the future. Collaborators produce electronic media. Its creation and ultimately its consumption are meant for groups of people, particularly in relation to the mass print culture of books. The development of the Internet, as the electronic media age enters its adolescence, is bearing this out.

The future bodes well for those in the Church who are willing to move beyond the AV mentality to create electronic media messages that interpret the Gospel to, and ultimately transform the listeners of, this new age. The first step in this process is the task of learning to think visually.

Broadcasting worship experiences: Is it necessary or even desirable?

Worship is the foremost corporate activity of the body of Christ, in which we "ascribe to the LORD the glory due his name" (Psalm 29:2 NIV). Jesus told the disciples that where two or three are gathered in his name, the Spirit would also be present. Acts 2 tells us of corporate gatherings marked by the apostles' fellowship and what Luke calls "the breaking of bread and of prayers," by which he means worship. The group worship experience is central to faithful life.

Television is merely an agent through which the experience of worship is taken to another time or place. That transport process, however, does not leave its message unchanged. Although the worship experience is replicated through the eye of a camera, it has been altered, because it is interpreted through the eye of the director, who must choose what of the entire experience to focus upon. Reception of the experience is now filtered through a gatekeeper, who is incapable of retelling the worship message in its entirety.

On the other side, there are the people who are receiving the worship service, often alone. Worship may also be an intensely personal experience, and certainly viewers are capable of experiencing worship singularly. (In fact, this is a primary understanding for the use of broadcast worship for shut-ins and faith community members who are disembodied from the corporate group. National televised ministries, so popular in the 1980s, operated out of the same assumption, and promoted the idea that has now mutated into Internet cyber-faith communities.) But studies have shown that broadcasts of church culture are ineffective at evangelism and discipleship. Any worship experience that a viewer might experience occurs outside of the support and accountability of a corporate Christian body. As John Donne said, "No man is an island." Broadcast worship cannot enhance a believer's experience of discipleship through interaction with a community of like-minded people, and so its only worshipful purpose is to enhance a believer's personal faith experience. For such a purpose, it is too expensive per person.

Shut-ins and those who desire a personal worship experience can be given a video or audiotape representation of weekend services every week for a fraction of the cost of delivering it live, as the live shoot requires production equipment, posting facilities, and airtime purchase.

Further, many existing communication forms do not translate to broadcast. Most traditional religious programming focuses on the transport of existing worship forms to a new medium. Much of Sunday morning church TV is based on shots of wood-laden sanctuaries, static rows of faces in robes, and a single person pounding out a sermon from a pulpit, with graphic overlays of Scripture for viewers to read along. Basically, it is the carrier of literate cultural forms into an electronic media age, or the shoving of round mouths into square screens.

In addition to the hindrance of such alien surroundings, sermon givers are further inhibited in that public speakers are no longer trusted in society. This is because oral communication is no longer the primary media form. It doesn't have the legitimacy and respectability associated with mass print and broadcast television (and soon, the Internet instead of mass print). Most viewers are disconnected. Adding pictures of the inside of the church building won't change that.

The solution? Storytelling has once again become the communication form of choice for the culture. We must communicate through the narrative form. Effective broadcast messages must speak in the cultural language.

A model for the future: the magazine format

Since electronic media is a storytelling medium, its messages should be primarily narrative. Viewers are much more likely to stop channel surfing on more interesting visual narratives than what the dated oral model of preaching is able to deliver. These narratives aren't even necessarily sitcoms, but anything that is able to create a sense of drama through the use of the medium, whether that is sports, sitcoms, or political scandal. Broadcast church that is able to speak this form would not really be worship in the biblical, corporate sense, but it would certainly be capable of worshipful moments. In fact, that would be the goal, to engage the viewer, regardless of the history of church architecture, in an experience of God. Its highwater marker would be the serendipitous, transcendent moment that occurs when the narrative says something about God and life that is fundamentally true.

Its content would more closely resemble the news magazine show *20/20* than *The Hour of Power*. It would be visually interpretive. A thirty-minute weekly program would have a host in a studio, a central theme and metaphor, and various narrative segments.

Other elements of church life, such as spots produced for education classes, could be featured. The goal is to engage an audience literate in electronic culture, whether they be churched or unchurched, by making a program that they wouldn't surf over.

Clips produced for corporate worship experiences would be adapted for broadcast; dramas edited, sermons highlighted in two-minute narratives with thematic music selections from the weekend functioning as background beds, much like a movie trailer.

Thinking visually

Every human creature is creative. To harness the creative spirit given by God is to become "non-linear." It means *not* sticking to the subject. It means that the random thoughts that pop in your head at odd times, such as prayer, may not be odd at all, but part of the work of the creative Spirit. A non-linear thinker recognizes and allows these thoughts to happen and is bold enough to verbalize them to others.

As the buzzword among the digerati in the early 1990s, *non-linear thinking* is the ability to think out of sequence.

Part of being non-linear means making liberal use of the brainstorming technique. Brainstorming is a technique best used in small groups in which random thoughts and responses are verbalized from a seed thought surrounding a particular topic. In brainstorming, there is no bad idea; all ideas are valid and noted. Brainstorming can be long and messy. It requires the total trust of all players. It also takes time to develop. Teams that have been together a few months are much more effective at brainstorming and generating creative energy and ideas than a team that has just begun.

Further, one does not need to be a creative "genius." The number-one rule for creativity: There is nothing new under the sun, and we have known that for thousands of years. For example, Western pop culture, which has become so self aware, it is now meta-culture; it is continually regurgitating itself.

Some say that the age of the multimedia database has stifled innovation, because performers have had the work of other performers always before them. I think it is the other way around. This age has democratized art. Now everyone has access to fine art forms formerly reserved for higher socio-economic classes with leisure time. But, instead of sustaining these traditional forms, the culture has created something out of its own experience. Imagery that sets trends has lost the tag of "fine" and has become "pop." Fine art connoisseurs say the latter isn't even art at all, it is too common, but that is the beauty of it, and a reflection of the God-image with which each human is born. This meta-state is not a bad thing. Out of so much borrowing is rising a new form of creative experience that gleans from a higher electronic media literacy, using the same creative ideas packaged in fresh ways. Electronic media is giving each of us the chance to become artists.

So you don't have to be a creative genius. Just remember two things: (1) be a student of the culture and (2) be adaptable. A student of the culture is one who is constantly in tune with TV, film, and the Internet. More than just a couch potato, though, a student of the culture watches TV critically.

Put down this book for a while and turn on the tube.

As you surf, pay more attention to the commercials than the programming. The thirty-second ads contain the true innovation. Where else will a company spend millions of dollars for the opportunity to spend less than a minute convincing you to purchase their product? Sounds crazy, but we know it's true. And to pull it off, they hire producers who understand how to speak the language. There's no better lab anywhere.

Remember that fluency means both adapting media trends and making media trends. One trend is the pace rule. Never take too long to say any one thing; keep the camera moving and the edits abrupt, because we are the attention-deficit generation. The flip side of that, however, is the old-fashioned idea of anticipation. The most effective media may be that which, within the quickened pace, enables us to pause and reflect for a moment. Cameron Crowe, director of *Jerry Maguire* and *Say Anything*, said, "Reflect, don't let Hollywood dictate the influence on culture. Move to the lead, then pass it." Of course, being able to effectively set new standards requires a strong grasp of the existing standards.

While surfing channels one afternoon I came across a show called *Bill Nye the Science Guy* on the local PBS affiliate. This show excels at portraying complex concepts of science in easily understood ways to reach youth. How can the unique Bill Nye concept be used in a ministry context?

The result for me was a call–to–worship video that illustrated a biblical metaphor, which is no longer part of our everyday culture, in easy to understand ways.

To be adaptable means to redeem an idea for use in a ministry context. Shaky text is a current trend in video that stemmed from the credit roll of the film *Seven* (1996). Although the movie itself, about a serial killer that takes his modus operandi from the seven deadly sins, is dark and not recommended, the opening credit roll struck me in its powerful use of imagery and text that couldn't sit still. The text treatment from that film was intended to create a state in which the very frame itself, the foundation of the picture, was about to come apart in chaos. I appreciated the chaos metaphor, and decided to adapt it to a TV spot for local multi-market cable for Christmas.

The spot contrasted the chaos of busy lives to the peace of the Christ child.

Of course, no one knew that this video spot was in response to a profane source. Some metaphors are redeemable.

An excellent way to track visual thoughts is to keep a storyboard journal.

Get a small bound notebook, or the sketch pad on your electronic PDA, and draw 4:3 squares. Leave it next to your remote. When you see inspiring ads, sketch them out. This will become a handy reference for conceptualizing video later.

For more information and ideas for thinking creatively, see the section in Part Three on building creative teams (page 79).

A persuasive medium

Video as a medium informs (provides focus) and persuades (provides hope), but the former is a function of the latter. Video is primarily a persuasive medium. It is best used to convey an idea with emotion. As a multisensory form, electronic media has more physiological power than any single form individually. TV by itself is *multi*-media, because it combines images and sound.

Despite what I heard in school, in this post-*Network* age it is difficult to argue that there is objectivity in any form of media.

The gatekeeping function of creating electronic media is now assumed.

TV news, by its very clipped nature, forces opinion and editorial comment. Watch the lead story of the six o'clock news on three different channels to see what I mean. O. J. Simpson looked a lot less like a criminal on the cover of *Newsweek* than he did on *Time*. Without placing political or ethical judgments on the gatekeepers, you realize that the bite is the essence of this form. You'd better make your point quick before I hit my remote.

In this context, information is best suited to text. This means that during announcement time in worship, tell the story on video and give the details in the bulletin. And during the administrative board meeting, visually introduce to whom the money is going, and give the figures in the line chart that can be analyzed.

Interpretation

Using electronic media in a multisensory environment means saying the same thing that is being said in other media, but in a unique way. This is the non-linear approach.

Don't try to visualize content that is best communicated orally. If you've painted a word picture in a sermon, don't settle for putting up that picture. Let the oral medium do its thing, and then do the visual thing: Say the same thing a different way. To illustrate Jesus' parable of the man and his bigger barns, you might create a series of images in which sections of a house are added sequentially: the suburban real estate deal being the boomer version of more grain.

In planning event media, continually ask, What things work best for graphics or video? What cannot be said another way?

How might a teaching be interpreted to electronic media? Many church-based educational curricula are developed around a book or a series of studies. Video might be used to support an argument presented in the text, or used to set up a theme or a metaphor for the argument. Research on the Internet can reveal quantitative information about cultural attitudes, or historical responses relating to the argument. There are many possibilities. Education in electronic culture is much more "object-based." A curriculum might consist of many different objects of varying communication forms: a book, a video and study guide for storytelling to and within the group, audiotapes for reflection later, use of the Internet, or an on-location video illustrating or interpreting the theme.

Watch late-night TV for one week, especially the parts before it turns into a talk show.

How do Leno and Letterman engage the audience visually? Do they use video clips, and if so, What do they say? How do they work?

Learning curve in making electronic media

As in Paul's admonition to the Corinthians that they must first drink milk, not eat solid food, it takes developmental time for creating effective electronic media in worship and education. It takes time to master speaking in a totally different language. When I first began meeting with Mike Slaughter at Ginghamsburg Church for the purpose of integrating media into his sermon, he would preach his sermon to me, and then say, "Okay, what can you give me?" It wasn't an environment friendly to creativity. I suggested that we bring in a couple of other people to create a team atmosphere, to help stimulate visual ideas. Even Mike, who had used multi-image slide projectors in the 1970s while a youth pastor, had an understanding of electronic media, but he had a learning curve while adapting to preaching out of this new form. Preaching has now become transformed into a convergence of sensory experiences that combine images, video, film, and sounds alongside litanies, repetition, and exegesis. Expect a learning curve in teaching and preaching, which has long been protected by authority and tradition; this learning to let go is just as crucial as the process of learning a new cultural idiom.

The cost of learning a new cultural language in a community is often cited as a barrier to change. However, the early adopters have taught us how to become adept at funding the process on a shoestring.

During my years in seminary, my wife pursued her music degrees at Wright State University, a local state-funded institution. Those were lean years. Much of the money I made to keep going was from contract media work that came from people associated with the seminary.

The experience taught me a number of solutions to computer issues, but more important it taught me that there is always an affordable solution to a problem, even if nobody knows what it is yet.

"Whatever the problem, there is always a solution."

That rule has served me well in learning to speak the language of electronic media in church life.

Funding issues invariably fade away when you ask the "So what?" question. How does the use of electronic media enhance someone's experience of Jesus? How does it point them toward the person of Christ? If it is not helping persons to serve God and love their neighbors, then you might be looking at a "gee whiz" purpose for the resources, and that is poor stewardship. Media is simply a communication form for Christian truth, which builds community (a common language) among those who are committed to the good news of Jesus Christ.

Basic Guidelines for Building Visual Elements

In this section we get inside the practical tactics that are used by a media minister. These include guidelines for video production, examples of video techniques, and the purpose of metaphor. Though the subject of metaphor might sound like the pursuit of a literary critic who reviews printed novels, it is actually the bedrock tactic for media ministry.

The metaphor

The metaphor is the single most important element of media ministry design.

The metaphor is not the theme. The theme is a functional description of the primary message that is to be told. For a Sunday morning it might be God's grace, or for a discipleship class it might be God's covenant. The metaphor is how the theme is to be communicated, so that it can be understood or at least embodied through experience.

The metaphor is a tangible representation of an abstract idea.

The Bible depends upon metaphors. Every major theme represented in Scripture is communicated through a metaphor. The Holy Spirit is a dove, or water, the call of God is heard in the ordinary burning bush, God's covenant is sealed in the rainbow. Metaphors abound in the Bible because they are the essence of oral communication. Prophets such as Jeremiah spoke of a potter and his clay to represent God's continued relationship with an unrepentant Israel, and Zechariah talked about a flying scroll in an apocalyptic vision, in which God sends out a curse rebuking the captive Israelites for not keeping the Law. Even in the early church, leaders realized the value of the metaphor. Clement of Alexandria advocated the use of symbols such as doves, fish, a musician's lyre, an anchor, or a "ship running in the wild."

Read the Bible as a communication document. Notice all the times and ways God uses creative communications in indigenous language to lead God's people.

The metaphor may be a phrase or an entire sentence, but it is often object-oriented, or at least a combination of the two. Metaphors are all around us, but we notice that a metaphor is "dead" when it is over-used (trite) or becomes a function of literal speech. In his parables Jesus used objects that people perceived each day, such as the staples of an agrarian society: a mustard seed, a woman with a broom, workers in a field, yeast, a banquet feast, and so on. In seeking the metaphor, ask the question, To what does the theme compare? Again, the theme is an analytical, propositional, or functional description. You pursue the metaphor through the imagination of what and how it is to be told.

Don't give up on applying metaphors. It is not always easy, especially when working with persons who are conditioned to create themes in propositional and abstract form, which is the methodology of the print culture. But time and again I have seen that the effectiveness of a presentation is directly determined by the effectiveness of the metaphor that communicates the theme.

Examples of new media in worship

To get a taste of media ministry on a typical weekend, here I outline a number of possibilities for what a media ministry might pursue:

1) Film and video clips to set up a theme

Consider these resources:

- *The Source*, Zondervan Publishing House, Grand Rapids, Michigan, (800) 876-7335
- Creative Assistant, Seeker Solutions, www.seekersolutions.com, 1-888-867-7369
- The best source for films, though, is a team of movie buffs and an Internet movie site such as www.MrShowbiz.com.

Use, but don't abuse, film clips. Keep them fresh, and not typical. Avoid reuse. A well-placed film clip ignites many services, but like anything else, weekly use will kill its spark.

2) B-roll behind a speaker. This might be news footage from the local station, environmental shots establishing a locale or setting, or shots of a person, event, or place.

B-roll: accompanying video footage depicting a voicetrack. B-roll comes from the B-reel, or the cutaway reel in editing suites

3) Chroma-keying, or the combination of graphic images over live camera images. This is effective for reiterating a point or message during a sermon. (This requires a video mixer. See Part Four, page 111, for details.) This is also known as "supering," or "lower-thirding."

4) A speaker's points, which might be illustrated with still graphics or 2-D or 3-D animations.

 QuickTime is computer video format that works well with graphic images in presentation programs such as PowerPoint. Small QuickTime videos may be combined with graphic images to create moving type, for example.

5) A series of graphic images, such as a slide show, behind a song. For example, a song about outreach might include snapshots of a church group in mission.

6) Looping video behind song text, or prior to the event, or mixed with live shots, or graphics during a featured musical selection, to help establish a mood.

7) Video or animated transitions between event elements. During a worship service it is the transitions that most frequently lose people. One person finishes, and it takes an eternity for the next person to get up on the platform to start. Video transitions can fill the gap while reinforcing the message.

8) A series of stills in a sequence, to simulate motion.

9) Graphic illustrations and interpretations of Scripture readings, Scripture references, sermon illustrations, announcements, prayers, monologue, and dialogues.

Producing Video: The Principles

There are five basic categories or subgenres on the "short-form" video spectrum, which can be mixed in many ways by a media minister:

• Advertisements, within and external to church life;
• Faith moments, or discipleship-building segments,

including testimonies, or ways in which spiritual maturity is modeled;

- Worship support, through the use of a metaphor to establish a theme;
- Mission moments, telling stories about the church's stewardship of resources;
- Narratives, or video storytelling, such as soaps and sitcoms; these are the hardest to do.

After you have chosen a genre for your ministry video clip, there are five critical principles for producing incredible ministry video:

1. Content is king.

I frequently read trade magazines to stay abreast of creative and technical innovation in the media ministry. Often, I am struck by advances in technology that precede gaps in the communication process. This intuition was confirmed one day when I received a trade magazine issue with a byline in big type that read "Content Is King!"

Of course, content is king, the most important aspect of the production. Don't get a misplaced determination of the importance of a clip because of its production value.

Ask the "So what?" question at least three times over the course of planning and producing a video clip. Variations of the question include:

a) What if we don't show it?
b) What is it really saying, and how well does the video communicate?
c) How does it add to the experience of the event?

Just as untrained writers tend to overdo **bold type** for emphasis, media ministers tend to get caught up in "toasterisms," or in the random, meaningless, deadly use of visual effects. One example is the use of video for messages that are not central to the event, because it reinforces to participants the confusion between the medium and its assumed messages of entertainment. Great media tells powerful, life-changing stories. It is conceived, planned, and implemented as a critical component of worship and discipleship. Like any other medium, it should not be used unless it is central to the experience of God.

2. An effective graphic or video clip makes one point.

Don't try to accomplish too much through a single media element, which are most effective when they communicate a single message, in a language that the listener can understand. (However, don't be surprised if the video-taped metaphor means different things to various persons, exceeding even what the creator intended.)

I made this mistake as a student. I had contracted to produce a promotional video for a student ministry organization at a local state school, Wright State University. The video was intended to *(a)* excite local churches about transforming the lives of college-age students, *(b)* increase funding for student-focused ministries, *(c)* recruit students to be a part of the organization. Obviously *(c)* did not go with *(a)* or *(b)*, and I was unable to establish the "point" of the piece.

The now clichéd business axiom, Less Is More, applies. Electronic culture has shortened our attention span. Now, we *all* collectively have Attention Deficit Disorder. Choose one central theme, and explore it. Breadth is bad; depth is good. Depth may also be achieved through the use of other media. Depth is the purpose of multimedia. For example, a teaching series could use the video clip for a testimony, a printed guide for the study, classroom discussion as interactivity, and a hunt via a web browser for more information on a subject.

3. The big picture.

Ever notice how easy it is to get so involved in a creative act that you forget what it is like to be the viewer?

Keep the big picture in focus, both figuratively and literally.

A proper perspective helps to reorient the important and not-so-important details of a production. One viewer perspective is that shorter is always better. Good rules of thumb for program length are:

• Announcements and worship video pieces: one to one and a half minutes.

- Feature worship/event pieces: two to three minutes.
- Non-worship program pieces for education and small group applications: three to five minutes.

4. Video is for persuasion, not information.

Visual images do not analyze. They tell stories. Therefore all video is persuasive because it requires multiple hooks to have an impact on the senses. With music and voiceover, videos inspire the senses. Information that needs to be communicated, then, often is best done in multiple forms. Movie trailers at the theater prior to a film or at home with surround sound get viewers excited. Those same viewers know, though, that to get information about the film, the best method is to look in the newspaper, call the box office, or check on the Internet. There is a distinct difference between informative and persuasive mediums. Video is persuasive in that it establishes the setting and creates emotional connections, drawing viewers to a point of action, which may then be communicated in more detail through text.

5. Not all video is created equal.

Clips serve different purposes at different times. Sometimes a little piece is more appropriate as a support mechanism, and at other times a stand-alone piece is more appropriate. In worship, support pieces may introduce a character or situation that is then acted out in live fashion, through drama, monologue, testimony, or music. In other situations a story is best communicated in a feature fashion, which stands alone.

A Quick and Easy Guide to Video Production

Pre-production

- Figure out the audience.

Video producers, whether at the network, on the freelance beat, or operating a media ministry within the church, have clients. A client, even if a ministry representative, is the person with the message. The producer is the interpreter, assisting the client in translating the message into an effective visual form. Most of the time this does not mean copying the client's ideas to videotape verbatim, because these ideas may be misdirected, if they're not developed through proper questions put to the client. (The producer is a diplomat, who may be getting the client to agree that he or she has an ambiguous message.) Some of the questions include:

• What is the message?

Again, be very clear about a specific message. And stick to it.

• Who is the audience?

The worship venue dictates a different style for presentation than does a meeting, or a lecture in the classroom. The worship video may be celebratory, or it may be required to fit within established themes for a particular weekend. Although all video is persuasive, this is particularly true for large events.

There is an inverse relationship between the size of the audience and their collective attention span.

• How many people will see it?

Is the video clip to be distributed or consumed simultaneously by the audience? Some things will work better in a group setting. Stopping the video for reflection, for instance, wouldn't work in large groups, but it may be appropriate for small group or individual viewing.

• Determine the hook.

Develop a hook, or root metaphor, that makes the video compelling. The hook in literature is sometimes called the recurring motif, or the broad mechanism that conveys the theme for the story. This may be visual or aural. Read the preceding section on Metaphor (page 52) if you are struggling to name a hook for a video clip. Furthermore, every video has a dynamic element that moves the other pieces along, which helps the hook to sink deeply into the viewer. The music bed often drives a videotaped montage, whereas stories are often driven more deeply by the interviewee's voice.

• Write it down and draw it out.

Sketch out your ideas as part of the creative process. Write a script and/or storyboard for visual ideas. It is always helpful to pen thoughts and ideas, and spend time in brainstorming sessions with creative people. Scripting is good for a developed plan (although invariably it changes depending on what the captured video footage produces).

Storyboarding refers to actually drawing out in little boxes (frames, or screens) how you imagine the video to look.

This is not necessary for some of what you want to do, but will be helpful for more program-oriented pieces, or as preparation for specific camera takes in time-sensitive

6

7.5

10

13

locations. For example, if given permission to shoot on government property for two hours, it would be wise to know ahead of time exactly how you'd like the images to look in a frame.

Production

• The A-roll, or the interview

Decide if interviews, or "talking heads," are needed. Pick people and schedule interviews. In some forms video is testimony-driven. That is, personal stories compose the bulk of the narration. Thus, interviewing may often be the foundation of shooting video.

voiceover—narration without accompanying video

In lieu of A-roll, voiceover tracks are common. An example of this is reporter commentaries in news packages.

• The B-roll, or the environment

Decide on B-roll and a time to shoot it.

B-roll is the term used for video clips to play over voiceover tracks, so the viewer has something more interesting than a single face at which to stare for minutes on end.

It can be anything related to the topic, and is often the illustration of the matching voiceover. Lack of B-roll in video kills momentum. In production, there's an adage that you can never have enough B-roll. Shoot many more shots than you would ever need. You'll thank yourself in post-production.

Post-production

• Pick the right music.

At Ginghamsburg we review the previous weekend services on Wednesdays. During one worship review meeting, I was chatting with a few teammates about the impact of a video from the previous weekend. We felt that the piece, a recruitment tool for the church's men's ministry, had been effective. Suddenly, the music person pointed out with pride, "Well, it's the music that makes it!"

Of course it was. Some of the best scenes in film history wouldn't have worked without a powerful score underneath. Scenes from *Rocky*, when Sylvester Stallone jogs to the top of the Philadelphia Museum of Art, or *Apocalypse Now*, when the squadron of helicopters attacks a Vietcong delta to the accompaniment of Wagner's *Ride of the Valkyrie*, were both dependent on the emotional impact of the musical score. As a designer of media, don't underestimate the power of audio in a video production.

But you must be discerning about musical selection. Watch TV commercials if you want to learn about the persuasive impact of music.

Try watching a few commercials without sound.

You may find that the meaning of the commercials you see is dramatically different. Good video requires effective shots and an emotional audio bed.

Remember that copyright applies, particularly for non-worship applications. That favorite song or jazz piece may not be legal. See the Copyright section in the Appendix (page 158).

It may be cost-effective to invest $200 in CDs containing copyright-free music that is designed for video applications. These CDs may be purchased in one of three ways:

- Needledrop, the studio practice of keeping large libraries on hand and paying publishers per use (costs which are then passed on to clientele). This is the most expensive route for churches.

- Buyout, or the permanent purchase of single CDs or libraries from a publisher, which gives the user all rights for reuse. This works for light church use, where all the selections aren't heard in the first month.

- Licensing, or a short-term buyout, usually purchased by the year. Most of the highest-quality libraries may be licensed. For heavy use, licensing may be the best church option, since a library can be squeezed dry and then returned to the publisher within a certain time frame.

Music production companies may be found in trade magazines and over the Internet. Most will forward a demo or sample CDs for perusal prior to financial arrangements.

- Log your footage.

Logging is the process of dictating all the shots recorded on tape, often with notations regarding width of shot, length, beginning time on the tape, quality, and a brief description. Logging becomes more necessary for the larger production, and it can be tedious. But it is a vital step in knowing what you have to work with, to ensure the best production.

- Choose your best shots and discard the rest.

Be extremely selective. Sometimes it is necessary to go through the painful process of leaving great stuff on the "cutting room floor" if it doesn't belong with the central topic of the video. Stay focused.

- Edit your piece together.

Be sure to compose and integrate computer graphics. See graphics for further detail on design.

Allow one hour for every minute of straight video editing, and at least twice that for graphics-intensive video. If you don't have your own equipment, various post-production houses in most communities have per-hour rates that include an operator. Many often provide off-hour times to non-profit clientele as a write-off. Another option is to check into cable access studios, which are available in many larger cities and offer mid-range quality equipment for public use. See Part Four for types of video editing systems.

• Don't forget distribution.

How will people see it? If it is in worship, then set up TVs or projection and make sure video plays back well and at good volume. If in homes, then make the appropriate number of copies.

Suggested Video Resources

Video Production Handbook, by Gerald Millerson

A basic guide with practical tips from a master of TV station culture. (He also wrote a tome full of technical know-how entitled *The Technique of Video Production*. The first is the beginner version to the second.)

On a Shoestring and a Prayer, by Doug Smart

A binder publication by NRB (National Religious Broadcasters), which covers some details of the narrative form of video.

Home TV

Watching TV at home critically, with attention to composition, shot sequence, edits, and graphic style, is one of the best ways to learn video. For training purposes, commercials are better than programming. Late-night talk shows and live performances on networks, such as VH1, are laboratories for instruction. Even features on star athletes before sporting events give stylistic examples of how to compose short-form stories.

Somebody else's stuff

If you think of something you've seen that fits the bill as well as something you could create, check into purchasing a copy with usage rights. Be tenacious. You'd be surprised how often copyright holders will accommodate your needs. I put calls to a number of local PBS affiliates around the country in search of someone to sell me a *Bill Nye* episode that would help me on a call-to-worship video clip. When I found the person, she was more than happy to sell me a copy of the tape and granted permission to use it in worship.

Caveat: a request for non-profit use doesn't go over well at commercial networks. Networks will likely never grant you permission to use anything they broadcast, because they fear illegal copying and reproduction of broadcast material and because broadcasters are tuned into the present use rather than the reuse of their footage. It is generally not worth the effort to approach them.

Other possibilities for pre-produced video clips include:
• Church Video Association, 703-590-0214
• Moody Video, 800-842-1223

How to Make Great Eye Candy

Graphics 101 : Computer Technology and Image Making

Computers vs. slide projectors

I can think of four reasons why you should invest in a computer system instead of producing weekly graphics with 35 mm slides:

• Time

Slides take time to produce. Even if you live next door to a one-hour slide making factory, that is one hour more than it takes for a computer to display an image. And when a worship deadline looms just ahead, an hour is an eternity.

• Money

Although a computer initially costs more than a slide projector, it requires no additional production expense (unless you simply must have that special upgrade). Slides require a weekly production budget, which can become expensive quickly.

• Flexibility

A screen of song lyrics cast onto a slide is a song permanently set. Computer-generated text may be changed at a moment's notice, which is especially helpful given worship leaders' frequent decision changes, and those unfortunate typos.

• Potential

Computer images handle not only photographs, the usual slide application, but they handle video captures, 2-D art and animation, and 3-D models. Graphics applications are not limited by technology in computers, only by the artist's imagination.

Getting images into the computer

See Part Four: Tools, Phase 4.

Work with a primary image for the event.

Represent the metaphor visually through a single title or headline graphic that may be used periodically to reinforce the theme. The title graphic should state the theme, either with imagery, text, or both.

Make it eye candy.

The CDROM illustrates a number of effective graphic styles and describes what makes each work.

Keep your graphics simple, bold, and fun to look at, but representative of television culture rather than computer culture. Television is our dominant cultural medium. Although forty-five precent of homes have PCs, ninety-nine percent have TVs, and over half are TV homes with multiple sets.

In other words, imitate the dominant culture of TV, not computer culture.

Use the forms of broadcast television rather than PowerPoint presentation pie charts. Choose primary colors over subtle variations. Keep with the small-box colors of

Crayolas, and use light and shadows (see below) to provide depth.

Establish a style.

Pick a style and use it consistently for the duration of the event. Choose a consistent color scheme and typography. Use it for Scripture, sermon points, and graphic images. Make it present throughout the event in some fashion. This is called establishing an identity.

• Color

As documented by psychologists, color has an impact on perception and retention, and therefore shouldn't be minimized. Cool colors like blue, green, and purple have a calming effect, while warms like red, yellow, and orange are more stirring. In fact, red has been shown in studies to increase pulse and breathing rates, and blue to calm them. Many colors, in fact, have connotations with subliminal effects. Red may be associated with desire, passion, or violence. Green may be money or materialism. Blue is often a spirit color, as is white. Red, white, and blue, of course, are good for Civil Religion Day.

Further, for screen use, high contrast is important, usually light text on dark or deep backgrounds. Good color combination examples include yellow on blue, orange on purple, and white on almost anything dark.

Again, for instruction, watch TV, especially local and national news programs, which make heavy use of graphics with bright, matching colors.

• Fonts

There are two basic types of fonts: display, or headline fonts, and copy, or body fonts. Display fonts are goofy and unusual fonts, and copy fonts are normal, often traditional, and never the twain should meet. It's not much fun to read a Scripture on screen in Cookie Cutter or Dodge City font, although that might be appropriate for the reference.

• Lead the eye

Western culture tracks movement left to right, top to bottom. This means that graphic elements need to be positioned and balanced accordingly. Don't put an image in the bottom right corner, facing to the right, as this will lead an eye out of the frame. For example, if the background image is a landscape with a mountain in the upper left corner, and a tree in the lower right corner, then text should be placed around the tree, middle and lower left, left justified, maintaining balance with the background.

The rule of thirds: A grid that divides the frame into 9 parts, like a tic-tac-toe board, for the purpose of composing elements.

Apply the rule of thirds, and make sure that the elements are distributed in even fashion.

• Space

Use a lot of space within and in between graphic elements.

Elements are each of the objects in an image, whether they be display headlines, images of any size, or blocks of text. Avoid visual clutter. Leave plenty of space for elements to have their being, and to insert additional elements and illustrations.

• Lines

Random elements may be brought together in a cohesive fashion through the use of lines and frames. For example, titles and points can rest on a semi-translucent bar. Or, absent a directional background image, a two-and-a-half-sided bar can corral the elements to the center third of the frame. A common example is the recurring trend in design to use thick black borders to create boxes for images and information.

• Crop images

Delete all the unnecessary data around a subject to focus the viewer's attention to the purpose of the image. This is particularly the case when using images for illustrations, such as a newspaper headline, or when picking one person from a crowd.

Also, don't crop people at their joints, for it is visually jarring. Leave headroom and space in front of profiled faces, to maintain continuity.

• Light and shadows

The primary technique that separates the amateur artist from the professional is the use of imaginary lights on the surface of the graphic, which creates corollary shadows. Light and shadows can give a solid color depth and direct the eye to the purpose of the image. Some programs have light-producing filters; blurring light and dark areas achieves similar results.

Graphics 201 : Advanced Graphics Tips

Here is a set of random tips for finding the subtle differences that separate the amateurs from the experts.

How do I know when to make an illustration into a graphic?

Always say the same thing, but in a different way. Realize that each medium has strengths and weaknesses, and that some things are best left to oral communication. Don't try to illustrate every word picture that a speaker offers, some of which are too minor or temporary to warrant imagery. Keep to primary points and illustrations.

How picky should I be about the timing of a graphic that is displayed behind a speaker?

Studies have shown that there are direct relationships between the timing of graphics and voiceover narration, and their impact on viewer retention. One study examined graphics that are timed in seven-second intervals preceding and following voiceover narration, up to twenty-one seconds in each direction. The results show that graphics synchronized with voiceover and graphics preceding the voiceover by seven seconds had a much higher retention rate for the viewer than those preceded by fourteen or twenty-one seconds or followed by seven, fourteen, or twenty-one seconds. The differences were as much as thirty percent in retention of the image for the viewer. So if the pressure of exactly matching an errant preacher's ramblings are too intense, err on the early side.

Should I add text in an image manipulation program, such as Adobe PhotoShop, or in presentation software, such as Microsoft PowerPoint?

There are advantages each way, depending on the particular software application. Most presentation programs are incapable of doing more advanced effects such as blurred drop shadow or glow, both of which are features of graphics from TV culture and not computer culture. These must be accomplished in an image manipulation program. But the latter are more difficult to edit in case of error. As a rule of thumb, only do main points, or the display font graphics, in image programs, as these are less likely to be edited. Then produce body copy such as Scriptures and song lyrics in presentation programs, which are easily changeable.

I can't take photographs, and I draw like my two-year-old. Is there any hope?

Fortunately for you, entrepreneurial artists had you in mind when they created resource libraries of images and art. These libraries consist of everything you'd want, from textured backgrounds to clip art and photo galleries. Most are relatively cheap, too. The Internet is a great place to find them. For a list, refer to Phase 4 (page 147).

Why cameras in church?

Cameras might be used in worship and teaching events in church life for two primary reasons:

First, cameras are functional. Many sanctuaries have a number of badly positioned seats, which might be defined as any seat more than fifty feet away from the platform. This is problematic because preaching, an oral form, relies heavily on the facial expressions and body movements of the preacher. Closer views are also necessary for dramas and skits, and liturgical elements such as baptism.

Second, there is a level of interpretation and meaning derived from well-composed visual representation. For an explanation, see the section on cameras (page 149).

Fear not!

Be willing to take risks. Be willing to try new things, and learn from layout trends in periodicals and television. Be tenacious in the face of miscues and naysayers. Some people will never get the vision, and others only when it is done right. Be willing to fail in order to achieve, and never give up on your vision. Change never comes without resistance.

> ### Dealing with negative people:
>
> Naysayers want a fight. They don't want to engage in dialogue. They want you to become a naysayer, too, because then they've won. Follow the advice that has been the mantra of presidential aides for generations: "Never complain, never explain." Just cast vision. Tell positive stories of change and transformation. When people begin to get negative, to quote a colleague of mine, "just don't go there." Be a yes-sayer. At all times, edify.

This is a media *ministry*. Media produced for the Church is part of God's larger mission to the planet, so trust what the work of the Spirit can do. One church trusted God's desire for people's gifts to be used for the purpose of the Kingdom, and mobilized a group of junior high youth to create video for inside and outside their church community. The children called themselves Vid-Kidz. Given freedom, the kids are doing incredible things with the internal church communications and community outreach. Their efforts include a mission-awareness project in which VidKidz used cable access equipment to do a series of "On the Street" interviews during the local community's 1998 March for Jesus rally. Pastor Ken Dewalt says that the biggest part of the story is that their church is a recent start-up, with an average attendance of fifty-eight. He says,

We often get the question, "How can such a small church support so many small groups and cool stuff like VidKidz?" Any church that decides to be a permission-giving church can do it. Letting go, and letting God, never meant more to me than it does after serving here for my first year and a half. And someday we'll be able to move from overheads to PowerPoint in worship because we asked our kids to take over the mixing boards and the video cameras!

There are groups of people in your church, many young, itching for the opportunity to use their creativity and gifts in design and production for something meaningful. Because media literacy is innate in younger generations, God will provide the creative and the technical means to accomplish the mission that God has set forth.

Part Three:
Building a Championship Crew!

Don't do this alone. Don't even try.

O n a vacation to the Florida Keys, I visited the home of Ernest Hemingway, which since his death has been turned into a museum. Part of the tour led me by his writing studio, a loft apartment with walls of books, two or three chairs, and a single desk. The tour guide said that while in Florida, Hemingway wrote all of his books in this room. It was a quiet, isolated room, obviously meant for one person, alone with his thoughts.

Compare that to the studios I encountered while an intern at CBS Television City in Hollywood. One night while there I witnessed a live production of the *Tom Snyder Show*, which aired following Letterman at 12:30 A.M. EST. Eight people sat in one small room, many talking simultaneously, limbs and chairs bumping. These "authors" were practically sitting on top of one another! This creative environment was not a space for Hemingway, to be sure. However, each person in the crew served a particular purpose and was critical to the success of the production, which was being watched by literally millions of people across the continent. The same was true for many other productions that I witnessed, including sitcoms, original television events, and feature films.

Team-oriented production is central to electronic media. The church is losing relevance in our culture partly because it continues to put all of its weight on one central leader. Although ministry in the age of the printed word was largely individual, ministry in the electronic age is like a television studio, operating with a number of specialists, who accomplish more than would be possible by a single author, no matter how gifted. Electronic media authors are now able to create more with less than mass print authors because of the coordinated efforts of teams. Developing effective teams for both the creation and presentation of electronic media in church environments will be the key to success for media in ministry.

Establish the Game Plan

Importance of unpaid team members

The crew of unpaid people is at the heart of an effective ministry. Ministry for the electronic culture is not about what staff to hire to accomplish the tasks at hand. It is about empowering laypersons to utilize their gifts in ways they never thought possible for the purpose of advancing God's kingdom.

You will discover that as the media ministry develops, it becomes an entry point for people previously not part of the church community. Because of the opportunity to utilize their gifts and talents, individuals will join the team and become regular attendees at the church. Like the movie *Field of Dreams,* once you build it, people will come. A couple of years ago I asked a film student at a local state college to create a two-minute promotional piece to recruit people to the sound ministry. The student, Dave, got three friends from campus to help him make the spot. None were a part of our church community, but following production of the spot, two of the three became regular attendees!

The temptation, once you have discovered talented, committed people, is to pay them, to ensure that your team will not collapse on some given weekend. But relationships get a bit complicated when a team becomes a mix of paid and unpaid people, for a number of reasons. The addition of money, especially with Christians who are young in their faith, can obscure motives for services given, and interfere with their growth in giving as an expression of faith. As Cordeiro states, the act of serving is not so much about what the servant is doing but rather who they are becoming.[1] Paid persons have a tendency to hoard knowledge as a form of job security. Paying servants can also lead to the game of secret keeping—does director #one, who is paid to direct, know that director #two is not paid? If so, then does director #one suddenly begin having an inflated sense of importance regarding his/her work in the ministry? Or if not, then does director #one make the mistake of telling director #two about the payment? Such knowledge would obviously hurt efforts in building community. Further, paid staff is no hedge against missed deadlines or failed projects.

The motive of an unpaid person is never in doubt.

One of the two young film students who came to our congregation during the production of the spot, was given the opportunity to become part-time staff to handle the increase in demand for media in education. Although he was an excellent unpaid team member, the expectation of being paid staff was too much at that stage of his faith journey. After a year in that capacity we removed him from a job that did not fit him. He returned to his unpaid role, and since has excelled as a director with strong technical skills.

For the first three years of media ministry at Ginghamsburg Church, as the church tripled in size, I was the only paid media staff person among an unpaid team of ninety people. Through that team we accomplished great things and set the stage for our current mix of paid and unpaid team members. It is through unpaid people, pursuing their gifts and talents in ways they never dreamed possible, that a media ministry can transform lives and build the Kingdom.

Establish a goal

For what purpose will your teams be working? Do you wish to coordinate electronic media into the worship context, or education, or both? Will the media you create be a part of your community experience once a month? Every week? These questions must be answered before you can begin.

Answer the following multiple-choice question: I am . . .

__ A media professional bringing this exciting communication tool to the life of my church

__ An amateur with tons of creative ideas eager to use this tool in the life of my church

__ A print culture geezer who doesn't see the need for electronic media in the first place.

The challenge of media professionals in church life is to act out of what you have, not out of what you don't have. Regardless of the quality of the media equipment available at your disposal, it probably will not compare to what a professional studio has. But take heart! The tools for making electronic culture are becoming democratized. The landscape for media is changing drastically as home systems become powerful enough to accomplish digital media creation. (In fact, it is likely that one day a central home appliance will be the production and distribution center for all electronic media applications).

Recently, a twenty-something in California created a satire called *Troops* (a ten-minute hybrid of *Star Wars* and the TV show *Cops*) with a home system that was so effective it received national attention, and the feedback of *Star Wars* creator George Lucas. I downloaded it from the Internet. The quality of the short film is amazing. The lesson: do not underestimate the creative power of media creation for local church environments, regardless of supposed technological limitations.

The challenge for amateurs, on the other hand, is to not bite off more than you can chew.

 Remember that mediocre media is worse than none at all, because it doesn't communicate.

Mediocre media distracts. So do what you can, and do it well. Your creativity, and that of your team, will be such that you want to try great things. Risk-taking is part of the makeup of any media guru, and the only way to grow, but always pass those risks through the test of excellence. It's a difficult balance to maintain.

Create a culture of koinonia

koinonia: The harmonious fellowship of believers who share a common mission.

Koinonia is a New Testament word that is variously translated as "fellowship," "sharing," or "partnership." It's the experience of harmony through Christ that can happen when a community of Christians works together for a common goal. You don't have to make it happen as a leader, either; it is a gift from the Holy Spirit. Your function is to provide the freedom for the expression of this gift, and to encourage team members' passion when the gift is apparent. One way to energize the team is to constantly cast stories of transformation in the lives of people who attend the church.

Electronic media plays a role in individual transformation, as well. About two years ago at Ginghamsburg Church I produced a worship segment telling the testimony of a young couple coming to faith. The video story, like no other medium, described a couple heartbroken at the loss of their newborn baby, but held up through the love and support of the church community. A few months after that worship experience, I witnessed how media were not only using their story to inspire others, but were actually inspiring them as well. At a later worship service, we closed with video and audio of ultrasound from an unborn baby being carried by the preacher's wife. The sight and sound of that unborn baby on the big screen were a cathartic experience for the grieving couple. Of course, emotions are complex, and the opposite could have happened; the point being, media resonates, and elicits reactions in viewers. Media is not the communication form of a stagnant church. It will cause change and growth. It will jerk your congregation out of their apathy and indifference.

As your church grows, relay stories of life-changing work to the team, and make sure they understand their role in transforming the community.

Qualities to look for

People who catch your vision

More important than technical mastery is the condition

of the person's spirit. Sometimes a little technical expertise without an understanding of the vision of the ministry can be dangerous, particularly when you are forced to rely on individuals with a greater degree of technical knowledge than you have.

It is very important in a team environment to have technical accountability.

Don't just let the people loose, because ultimately they are not responsible for the care and use of the equipment.

There's nothing worse than a carefully planned and produced service ruined by an over-tweaked projector or soundboard. **(See pre-worship checklist on confirming all the details!)**

Soft skills and hard skills

It is just as important to have leaders and administrators in the ministry as it is to have technically apt people. I specifically recruit non-technical people and train them because it is easier to teach video skills than it is to teach people skills.

In *Doing Church as a Team*, Wayne Cordeiro says that when you're starting a ministry, your first step is to recruit four leaders.[2] Keep those four leaders within your care, no less and no more, for the duration of the ministry, regardless if the community is ten or three hundred people. These four people will be the heart of the ministry and will raise a team strong in number and spirit beyond what you could accomplish single-handedly.

These leaders don't necessarily have to fit the ministry's needs by function or role. The job of the ministry director is to take their mix of gifts and apply them in whatever way best fits the team, as the coach adapts his team's strategy based upon the strengths of the team's players. As to who these four people shall be, they are the four who exhibit the most passion for the ministry and have the best ability to articulate their passion and lead others.

Technical proficiency

Every church has introverts with great computer and video skills. This ministry is made for them. Although not necessarily your leaders, they are the ones who will be able to step in immediately with the skills necessary to get the ministry running. Many people are visual learners (hence the need for media ministry!), and will only see the power of media in communicating the Gospel by seeing it in action. When these techno-geniuses put on the initial worship experiences, possibilities will become evident and others will come. They can then become your trainers as you bring in other people to grow the team.

The Servants in a Media Ministry

Basic organization

Media ministry may be organized into any number of teams, depending on church size. One possibility is three teams: video, sound/lighting, and tape duplication. The first two teams function between worship and education. A typical production might require a crew of about ten: six video, two sound, one lighting, and one tape duplication. The ministry would then be structured on a weekly basis, with different crews serving a particular weekend of the month, all weekend. Schedules are established, with as little variation as possible, to ensure that each crewmember always knows the particular time and date he or she is to serve. All team members serve the entire weekend, including Saturday rehearsal and worship, and Sunday worship. Having one crew for a weekend prevents constant rotation of positions, which can make each worship production equally weak! Although team members are caught up in the details of production, making it difficult to actually worship the weekend that they serve, their commitment is for that weekend only, leaving them free to worship without distraction the other three weekends of the month.

The schedule remains fixed, ideally, but there is naturally a small rate of turnover, as media can develop into a large volunteer ministry. So there is a continual need for team members. Conduct training workshops periodically, alternating between team functions.

Area of expertise

Have each media ministry member choose an initial area of expertise. This self-selection does not encourage exclusivity; rather, a method of specialization enables everyone to serve in specific, needed ways. Media ministry is not like writing a book; it requires the skills and talents of several gifted people, working in cooperation for the good of the whole.

Although the area of expertise is that which requires your team members' primary attention, have them be aware of processes in every area, as knowledge is cumulative and creates a better working team environment. Empathy and understanding are crucial to an effective ministry; a functioning knowledge of the entire media ministry enables this to happen. The best leaders are the ones who have experience at every level of operation. Team leaders are much less likely to call for the impossible or create tension out of ignorance if they understand the demands on the other team members.

Committing to serve

Encourage team members to realize their commitment to serve in the media ministry, before they decide to join because it is "cool." Electronic media is intrinsic to worship, and team members are a vital part of the process. When a new visitor walks in, one of the first and most lasting impressions will be what is displayed on the big screen of the wired church. Our task in ministry is to create and present excellent electronic media to communicate the message of the transforming power and love of Jesus Christ. We want that first impression to be a good one, and subsequent experiences to be of effective communication through minimal distraction. Thus, their trustworthy participation is necessary, and the media ministry could not function completely without each member's presence and dedication to ministry tasks. Part of that commitment means abiding by certain norms, which are suggested as follows:

• You are expected to serve when scheduled. If you cannot serve, then you are expected to inform your team leader at least twenty-four hours in advance. We understand that there are times when you will not be able to serve when you are scheduled, but please make an attempt to give the team leader as much notice as possible. In lieu of a team leader, contact the coordinating staff person.

• We are a voice of encouragement. Never, in the intensity of live production, let your commitment to excellence outweigh your love for one another.

• Correction is to be done in a loving and caring way. We can fix anything that goes wrong with the equipment, procedures, and/or processes we use in media ministry. Repairing a broken heart can take a long time.

• You are expected to follow the rules of the ministry.

• You are expected to work the assignments/tasks you accept.

• You are expected to serve at least one weekend per month.

• You are expected to attend three worship services per month; a steady diet of worship is important to your spiritual growth.

Creative teams

Who do you get for your creative teams? Warren Bennis, in his book *Organizing Genius: The Secrets of Creative Collaboration*, outlines the characteristics of good creative teams:

• Numerous young players, with a couple of veterans to provide wisdom. Younger people do not have the same sense of failure that older people have.

• More generalists than specialists; people who always see the big picture.

• A strong leader; someone who can provide general direction and draw out creativity and coherence in the thoughts of others.

• A constant goal or deadline, which forces creativity, but not perfection. Such a goal might be a weekly worship service or a fall education series.

• A sense of divine mission, that they have been called by God to this time and place for this purpose.[3]

Keep your mission focused. Know precisely the purpose and limits of your project. Keep resources handy. Know how to research, as well. Much information comes indirectly; for example, there are no references in the Bible for use of electronic media, but one can find many passages regarding language, communication, speaking, and writing (such as James's admonition on the power of the tongue). Or, try acquiring a film still from an older movie that may not be at the rental store by checking film books at the library.

Inventor Stan Mason, the creator of disposable diapers and squeezable ketchup bottles, offers a few tips on creativity:

• Sketch it out. If you're having difficulty seeing something, a visual interpretation may help.

• While brainstorming, get ideas flowing to the point of saturation. In creative sessions, quantity can often produce quality.

• If you're stuck, go to lunch, and don't talk about it. Give the idea hibernation time. This may even mean sleeping on it.

• Furnish the right creative environment, whatever that means for your team. Decide as a group what your environment should look like and make it available. For example, set up plenty of space to move around and plan. Make sure the temperature is just right. Have food and drink available.[4]

Team roles

My "top seven" list of important media functions, in no particular order:

Camera operator
Activities include live production, under the director's lead, and field production for pre-produced clips.

Computer operator
Creates and/or operates computer system(s) to project images and animations onto the screen during live events,

which includes text for praise and worship songs. (See the Design section, page 37.)

Technical director
Operates the mixer through which the various sources of video are mixed for projection.

Director
Works with all team members (including audio and lighting) and the speaker. The director is the leader of the crew and gives the commands to other operators on the headset system.

Sound
Operates live sound events, including set-up, gain, equalization, and mixing.

Lighting
Programs and operates the lighting board for live events.

Tape
Audiotapes live events; makes copies of these for sale and distribution.

Team-building tips and techniques

Build depth

The introduction of a media ministry in church life, particularly in worship, is one of the more demanding challenges among all the possibilities emerging in electronic media culture. Even television sitcoms take a thirteen-week break every summer, but worship occurs fifty-two Sundays per year. The best way to avoid burnout is to build depth within the team. As a coach, spend a percentage of your time each week building teams, even if this cuts into your personal production schedule. I spend on average ten hours/week in relationship building and training. A team with depth can better handle the transitions of life and continue to move ahead in ministry. The alternative is a small remnant who are asked to carry the whole ministry forward, and ammunition for naysayers who resist change and growth.

Media ministry is a complex hybrid of existing styles of electronic communication. It is not broadcast television, certainly; it is not PowerPoint for the office, it is not home videos of the backyard cookout. Its purpose is not to entertain. As a new, interpretive communication tool, it requires adaptability through which unskilled people do not have to unlearn anything. They're moldable, without pre-conceived notions.

Although it's pleasant to have professionals at your disposal, often the most committed, highly trained team members are the ones with little previous experience, beyond a desire to learn about and serve others through a media ministry.

Cross-train

Move your team members, with their consent, every six to twelve months. Many people will get bored in a single capacity, and might leave the media ministry. Training them in multiple functions, or cross-training them, makes team breadth and depth greater. Don't rely on any one person too much.

Develop a farm system

Look for media venues outside of worship, such as youth and education functions, where the number of people gathered at any one time is fewer. These events become a farm system, a means of training and tracking the potential of future skilled players. Smaller functions provide an ideal hands-on training environment, while not sacrificing the quality of the primary event.

Rehearsals

As you begin to put together technical crews, conduct a series of technical rehearsals prior to "opening day," with a few people to witness the event.

A Guide to Developing a Skilled Media Crew

Videographers

The camera operator is the foundation of any video

team. The camera eye is the most often seen, visible ministry function of most media-equipped churches. When visitors enter the church for the first time in multisensory worship, the cameras are one of the primary elements that they notice. And an effective use of cameras may play an important role in the return visit of an unchurched person.

In a basic sense, the camera in worship serves as a viewing aid to those who sit some distance away from the platform, but when well composed and ordered, the camera brings meaning to the elements of a live event. It is thrilling to watch a carefully directed, intentionally chosen camera sequence during a live musical piece.

Camera operators must be smooth and steady. They must have a good eye for composing a shot, because the director doesn't have time to talk them through shot composition during the intensity of a production. They must remain calm, stay focused on the subject/object that they are shooting, be prepared to accept last-second changes, and smoothly execute transitions.

The tool: camera anatomy

There are three sections in most high-quality cameras: the lens, head, and the back end, which can be either a studio back or a docked field recorder. Two or all three of these sections may be combined in some less expensive camera models, which are called camcorders.

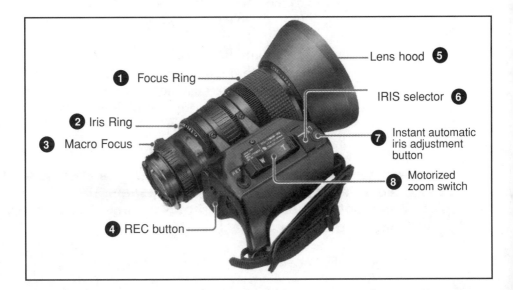

Lens

The lens is the cylindrical extension on the front part of the unit. It is actually a composite of a series of separate components.

Prop the book up while you read this section so you can investigate your camera at the same time.

Never clean the glassy part of the lens with your finger, as skin oils could scratch it. Obtain a special cleaner from your local dealer.

No fuzzies, or the many ways to focus

focus

The very front wheel of the lens is the focus. Only on the least expensive cameras does this have an automatic function. If you have one of these auto-focus cameras, find the guide to your camera and make the focus manual. Auto-focus is almost always a BAD thing. When there are multiple elements in a frame, often the camera cannot determine which is the focal point of your shot, so it will alternate back and forth. The camera is kindly giving equal time to the two elements, but you know better. It's implacable, too, so disable the autofocus feature, and focus it manually.

Manual focus is controlled either by adjusting the wheel to the left or right, or through a device allowing the operator to do the same thing from his/her position behind the camera. The latter, called rear cam control, is specific to studio environments. In the field, operators do not have rear camera controls.

Focusing is not as simple as it may seem. The amount of depth within a shot is variable, depending on the following factors:

• the distance of the object from the lens

- how far in the camera is zoomed (which is called focal length)
- the amount of light the camera sees (which is called *iris*)

A small amount of depth means an object may be in focus but surrounding objects of varying depth may not be; a great amount of depth means that objects of varying depths may all be in focus. The movie *Citizen Kane*, directed by Orson Welles, was the first film to exploit extreme focal depth. Everything in the film is in focus. It's quite simple, actually.

Rent the film and read on about the iris for further discussion about depth of focus.

How to focus: In most settings, especially those in which the object is of static depth (including most worship settings), zoom as tight as possible on the object, focus, then zoom out to the desired distance (e.g., medium shot). It's that easy!

In situations of extremely small focal depth, even certain contours of a person's face may appear out of focus.

In such a case, a general rule is to use the eyes of the subject as the focal point. If, when zooming out, focus is lost, the back focus may need to be adjusted. See back focus below.

macro focus

Your camera may be well suited for either close-up or extended shots, depending on what type of lens it has. Extended lenses are ideal for shooting long distances, which may occur when a platform is more than thirty feet away. The extended lenses, however, sacrifice the extreme close-up, or in screenplay language, XCU (the point at which an extended-lens camera may not be able to focus is sometimes one to one and a half feet). Capturing the XCU is the purpose of the macro focus. It is located about halfway back in many camera lenses. If your camera doesn't have one, don't sweat it. You won't use it much anyway.

XCU situations occur primarily in non-worship environments. In such a situation, use the macro wheel, which is often adjusted using a little screw. Pop it out, and adjust. In the event that the main focus does not seem to work correctly, it is possible that the macro zoom screw has been offset from its standard placement.

back focus

The rear part of some lenses is the back focus. If your camera doesn't have one, it is not a fatal problem. In fact, not having a back focus can be a good thing because the camera takes care of it automatically, which means one less element to tweak on a Sunday morning, just before worship begins!

The back focus alters what the camera perceives as the rear of the focal length, whose range may or may not be great, depending on all of the previously mentioned factors. If accurately set, the back focus should rarely have to be adjusted, except for a particularly desirable shot.

The ideal way to test the back focus is with the previously mentioned technique of zooming in extremely close on an object, focusing, then pulling out. If the object maintains its focus, the back focus is set correctly. If the object loses focus, it will need to be adjusted. Camera manufacturers make charts for this sort of thing. Ask your local dealer.

zoom, or finding those nose hairs

Directly behind the focus on most cameras is the zoom. Often zoom is controlled by a separate lever. Instead of "ZI" for zoom in and "ZO" for zoom out, the camera might have the letters "W" (Wide) and "T" (Telephoto). Triggering the lever forward (T) zooms in on the object; backward (W), moves away. Most levers are variable, which means that the amount of pressure applied to the zoom affects the speed of its motion.

Most commercial cameras have a manual zoom option. To see if your camera does, check under the lens for a switch. The servo switch, when turned off, lets you adjust the zoom wheel on the lens, for extremely fast ins and outs.

The mark of an amateur videographer is liberal use of the zoom. Too much zooming gives viewers a peculiar sense of queasiness.

Len's camera Rule #2:
When in doubt, don't zoom in or out.

iris

 Behind the zoom you might discover the iris, also known as the aperture or f/stop control.

You'll know you have found it if you see a wheel with a series of numbers (increments) ranging from 1.4 to 22, or C. The iris adjusts the amount of light that is being let into the camera. The effect of this wheel is visible—look into the front of the lens as you adjust the wheel.

Contrary to common sense, the smaller the f/stop number (indicated by an *f#*), the more open the iris is, therefore allowing more light into the camera. So, when the f/stop is smallest (about f/1.4), it lets in the most light. Its minimum opening, when "stopped down," is about f/22, or "C," for closed. Remember, the smaller the opening, the bigger the number.

 Adjusting the iris affects two things: the exposure, or brightness of the image, and the depth of focus. The more open (smaller number) the iris is, the more shallow the depth of focus.

Iris is either adjusted manually or automatically. Unlike focus, automatic is a good thing with the aperture. Light varies greatly from shot to shot, and it's almost impossible for a camera operator to keep up with all the changes. There's no need to be Supershooter, though; so let the camera do all the work. On occasion, it is necessary to switch to manual, e.g., when a subject is sitting in front of an open window, because the back light, or light coming toward the lens from behind the subject, is so great it will stop down the iris, making the subject a silhouette.

Many settings in live environments will be between f/2.8 and f/5.4, depending on available lighting.

Camera head

Some cameras are equipped with controls on the camera head itself. Although the specific features vary from model to model, here are a few basic features to use.

NTSC bars

NTSC supposedly stands for National Television Standards Committee. Most engineers will tell you it stands for "Never Twice Same Color."

Color bars are what you see every night on some broadcast stations. It is a series of vertical bars spanning the spectrum of colors, with black and white bars across the bottom, and is used by engineers to set up video equipment. With this feature on, the camera replaces the lens's image with color bars. This comes in handy for two primary reasons: for the engineers to configure various sources together and to record color bars to videotape at the beginning of field recording (which is beneficial for post-production and editing). For the latter, record at least fifteen seconds of color bars.

white balance

Almost all cameras have a white balance feature, with preset option(s) and one or two settable configurations. A preset white balance is often represented by a little sun (outdoor) or a little light bulb (indoor).

What is the purpose of white balancing? Because color is light-dependent, the nature of color changes in variable light conditions. The human eye, magnificently created, is so superb that these changes are made so rapidly and well that they are not evident. Since cameras are not so advanced as the human eye, they must be instructed as to what color white, or the composite of all color, is. Once the camera is set for white, it bases all other colors on the setting. Watch Uncle Bob's home video, where everything looks yellow. That's because the white balance, probably an automatic adjustment inside his camcorder, was incorrect. Yellow images are indoor images shot with an outdoor setting, and blue images are outdoor images shot with an indoor setting. See filters below for more details.

Thus, every week when cameras are set-up, operators must balance the white on the cameras.

Make a large white board out of shower wall material and use it to balance the white when configuring camera for stage use.

Hold it up at stage front center with the lights at their normal setting. Set the white balance according to your camera's manual. On many cameras the iris must be on automatic for it to open again after black balancing. If after balancing, there is no image, switch the iris from manual to automatic.

filters

The color of white is variable, depending on the amount and type of luminance.

All light has its own temperature, which in video is indicated by the Kelvin scale. Good-quality cameras have filters that aid the camera in determining what color white is. Most of these filters have three settings:

1, for 3200 K, or indoor

2, for 5600 K + ND (or a neutral density setting), or sunny outdoor

3, for 5600 K, or cloudy outdoor

These are listed on most camera heads, next to the filter wheel. Depending on the light setting in which objects are being shot, adjust the filter to the closest available Kelvin temperature setting before white balancing to achieve a truer balance.

Standard Kelvin temperature ratings for video:	
Standard candle	1930 K
Sunrise, sunset	2000–3000 K
Household lamps (25–250 W)	2600–2900 K
Studio tungsten lamps (500–1000 W)	3000 K
Quartz lamps	3400 K
1 hr after sunrise	3500 K
Fluorescent lamps (usually higher; use #3 filter)	3000–6500 K
Sunless daylight	4500–4800 K
Midday sun	5000–5400 K
Overcast sky	6800–7500 K

ABL

"ABL" stands for Automatic Black Level. Whenever the cameras are configured by white balancing, black is set as well. In white balancing, the camera determines black by a percentage relationship to what the camera decides is white. (Did you know that black video is not really black, but is 7.5 percent of white?) However, sometimes what the camera thinks is black may be either too bright or too dark (this may depend on the clarity of a projected image, as well). As an alternative, operators may try turning on the ABL switch. When on, the camera makes its own determinations regarding proper black level. Experiment during rehearsal, if necessary, but make sure that all cameras are consistently on or off.

gain

Video, like audio, is measured in decibels

Gain artificially adds luminance, or brightness, to the lens by pumping up the decibel level of the video signal being sent through the camera head. The trade-off to adding artificial brightness is a sacrifice in quality. With added gain, the image becomes grainier. This is especially noticeable with a 12+dB gain setting. Mostly gain is used in broadcast news situations where the primary goal is to capture an event, sometimes at a sacrifice in quality. Often cameramen don't have time or ability to set up artificial light, so they'll turn on the gain instead.

Operators should use as little gain as possible. It is only beneficial in emergency situations in which the image cannot be captured any other way. With the loss of quality inherent in projection systems, it is crucial to send a high-quality signal from the video source.

A trip to the zoo: zebra stripes

One day, a Japanese video executive was struggling with an effective term for a new video technology. To clear his head, he went on a safari. While there, he saw a zebra. He was so struck by this odd, striped horse that he named his video function after the animal.

Just kidding. Zebra stripes are not named after the zebra, but they do make stripes in your viewfinder if you have one. If the zebra stripe switch is on, and the viewfinder shows pulsing lines in certain areas of the image, these indicate where the image is too "hot," or where white is greater than 100 percent, at which point the lens loses detail and people become ghostly. The easiest cure for zebra stripes is to turn on auto-iris. If on manual, adjust down one or two f/stops until the stripes disappear.

Back end

Many industrial- and broadcast-quality cameras have a recording unit docked to the camera, which allows it to function as a studio and a field unit. The tops of most cameras of this type have common VCR-type buttons for tape control. Using these buttons, it is possible to watch what has been recorded to tape. This can be a dangerous thing to do, for the tape may roll back as much as ten to fifteen seconds more than desired, which means that crucial footage may be overwritten when the tape begins rolling again for the next shot.

A technique for preventing loss of valuable footage is to record nothing (e.g., hand over the lens or color bars) about fifteen seconds before stopping to review. After review, cue up the tape by playing until static appears after the end of the "nothing" segment. The camera will backroll to about where the hand begins, and no valuable footage is lost.

> Len's camera rule #8: Sometimes no picture is better than a bad picture.

Cameras *cannot* make up for poor stage lighting, and cannot shoot around objects that are in direct line of sight.

The technique: camera artistry

Anticipation

A good camera operator is one who successfully anticipates the action, whether from the floor or from the director's commands. If the subject of a shot steps out of frame, a good operator will smoothly follow to regain the frame. For worship, this may occur within dramas, or when a speaker bends down or suddenly steps to one side or another. If such an event happens, do not wait for the director's command (which will possibly be "FOLLOW—NOW!!!"), but smoothly adjust the camera to regain the frame. A good camera operator will set up shots on his/her own initiative. During music performance, for example, operators may quickly set up shots for the director's choosing when they're not being projected.

The art of composition

Each shot should make a point. The composition of a slot directly impacts the effectiveness of the larger production. Here are three bad scenarios to avoid:

- Too much to see in the picture equals an eye that is distracted and flits around but concentrates on nothing.

- Too little in the shot equals a loss in the viewer's attention.

- Worst of all, when there are no visual accents to grab the attention, the eye may wander.

With proper arrangement of elements so that the main subject stands out from the surroundings, audiences will remain focused on the subject. A well-balanced shot will have a settled, stable feel to it. The frame position of a subject can affect whether the picture looks balanced or lopsided.

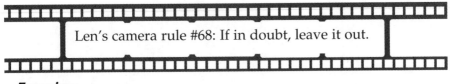

Len's camera rule #68: If in doubt, leave it out.

Framing

Most monitors and screens are adjusted to get the maximum picture size possible; however, all cut off at least a small portion of the outer edge of a shot—usually four to five percent.

Most projectors, however, display the entire image. What the lens perceives is what the projector displays. So be careful! Compose the shot to keep the important details within the "safe area" of the screen. Make sure to leave headroom; shooting a person so that the frame chops off his or her head, hands, or feet equals public-access quality video, which is to be avoided at all costs!

The safe area is the guaranteed portion that will show in a television or monitor, and is marked by a white box in many camera viewfinders. If there's no box in your little camera window, just imagine one, and don't put important material too close to the edges.

Keep a check on the distance between the top of head(s) and the top of the frame. If the headroom is too little, the frame will appear to crush a person and parts of head(s) may be cut off. If the headroom is too much, it puts the shot out of balance, which will distract the audience. Check with your presenters; they may not appreciate the perception of a squashed bug on the screen.

What's the best way to frame an image? The rule of thirds is an easy guide for placing subjects in the frame.

Simply compose subjects so that their weight is distributed along the lines that you created, or where the lines cross. Things to avoid:

• A horizon located halfway up the frame, as it is boring.
• A head in the center of the frame.

Example: A close-up shot of a "talking head" should be composed so that their eyes are on the top line. This puts the top of their head above the line and the rest of their body below. It uses enough of the screen without the atmosphere crushing down on the person. When positioned on the left or right third (with their nose on a vertical line), this is known as the "four-hanky" interview, which is useful for testimony clips!

It is often tempting to devise shots that are different (e.g., from a distorted perspective or using reflections or low angles). These shots are fine when created for a dramatic effect. But in many situations, unusual viewpoints don't merely make the picture look different; they draw attention to the technique and distract us from the subject. To break the rule of thirds, you've got to know it, and have a substantial purpose for your decision.

When framing shots, work with what you have. Don't ignore some of the elements in a frame to center on one or two. If it's in the shot, use it in framing the shot (e.g., your subject may be framed left center close-up, which is good, but if there's another instrumentalist behind him or her halfway off the edge of the frame, that's not good).

balance

Balance plays a greater role with multiple objects in a frame.

Grab your camera and try the following: First, position a large object on one side of the screen with several smaller objects on the other side. How do you compose the frame so that the eye is drawn to a specific object and the others don't interfere? Balance is a matter of relative size and distance from the center of the frame. Second, try framing the same subject from a different angle. If there are a number of separate items in a picture, they will look better when they are grouped in some way, rather than scattered around the frame. You can create the effect of unity in the picture, even when the subjects are some distance apart, by carefully selecting the direction from which you shoot them.

It is possible to vary the relative proportions and positions of elements in a frame by:

1. Adjusting the camera distance; the closer they are, the larger they appear.
2. Changing the camera height; the lower the camera, the more prominent the objects in the foreground become.
3. Changing the camera lens angle; using a wide-angle lens makes things rapidly diminish in size with distance.

Try composing a frame in which one object is very close and another is far off. Notice the disparate effect caused by such great depth.

perpetual motion

left to right

Remember that scene in *The Empire Strikes Back*, when Darth Vader is battling Luke Skywalker? Out by the bottomless donut-hole-thing, where Darth Vader chops off Luke's hand, Luke finds himself trapped. He is portrayed crouching in the lower right of the frame, with Darth Vader in the upper left.

Why are they positioned like that in the frame? Did George Lucas even think about that part? He sure did, and they are positioned like that because, as in most films, the hero is placed on the right side of the frame, and the villain on the left. Darth Vader, villain, was defeating Luke Skywalker, hero, so he stood taller in the frame. Higher up is good. When you want to portray triumph, try panning lower left to upper right, rising up to meet the hero!

 Our eyes are trained to read left to right. Engaging movement, then, is left to right in a frame.

leading

Always allow room for objects to move within a frame. For example, if a speaker is profiled in a frame, position him or her on the side opposite the direction they are pointing. This gives them room to move. It may be helpful to think of the speaker needing room to fill up a big talking balloon with all those thoughts.

Ditto for when he or she is moving. Give subjects leading room to move within the frame, so they don't appear about to jump off the edge of the frame.

shooting the action

Camera operators should be cognizant of the context of their shooting environment. What is the point of the production, and who is being featured? Always focus on the action in the environment. If it's the singer, focus on the singer; ditto for the guitar solo. When in multi-camera environments, there is usually a camera designated by the director as the primary camera. If the opportunity arises in this context, look for quick cutaways to other elements in the environment. See the Director section (page 105) for details on shot selection.

Len's jazz saxophone rule #1: If you make a mistake, act profound. The viewers may think that you are creating a new convention.

Preparation for worship

Here is a checklist for camera operators who are preparing for worship and other live events:

- Set up all cameras into the switcher. (Hopefully your video system is dedicated and does not move from week to week. Doing this every week could get extremely tedious. Little video parasites are known to inhabit nomadic video hosts.)
- Confirm the existence of a complete signal path. This means, turn on the camera and see the image on the projector. If no image exists, begin removing elements of the path individually until you discover the source of the problem. Keep notes as problems arise so that you can develop a troubleshooting checklist, and keep the checklist in a public space so that everyone has access to it.
- Once signal path is achieved, set the white balance in all cameras on automatic iris, and the right filter using full light.

That's it! You're ready to be a video artist!

Computer operators

The computer operator is responsible for the creation and or display of all graphics for worship and other live ministry productions. Graphic design and production are covered in Part Two and on the CD-ROM.

Switchers/technical directors

The role of technical director, often called *switcher*, or abbreviated as TD, is crucial because this person is the last stop before an image hits the big screen. The primary requirement for this position is a cool head. The TD must be able to operate the video mixer, without hesitation, in order to execute commands correctly and on time. On occasion, believe it or not, the director will lose focus or fall behind the pace of the production. The TD is the vice-president, self-responsible for swearing in and assumption of command. And in the horrible case that something goes wrong on the screen, it is the finger of the TD that must hit the mixer, and quick!

Here are some important roles for a switcher:

- The switcher works closely with the director during production, functioning as his or her fingers.

- In addition to making the actual choices for source input to the projector, the TD also keeps tabs on the quality of video coming from cameras, to assist the camera operators and the director if something is incorrect.

- The TD should have an accurate understanding of the video signal schematic (in other words, know which spaghetti cable connects to what meatball deck).

Gatekeeper: The decision–maker for the limited number of messages that may be transmitted through a given medium.

As it is the last stop before the big screen, the technical director also acts as a gatekeeper for what is projected. If for some reason the director is not aware of a quality problem, the technical director can add value by monitoring output for quality control. Contrary to what some may assume, the TD is more than simply a button pusher.

The switcher's tools

There are a number of specific technical pieces that a switcher may need to know, including the video mixer, routers, scan doublers, and projectors. The first obvious device is for mixing all the video sources together before heading to the projector.

Most church-level **mixers** are designed for no more than four input sources. When a facility outgrows these four sources, it is necessary to add **routers** to the spaghetti, which expand the number of possible inputs.

If you stare close enough at the TV, as your kids do, you will notice that the image, instead of being solid, is actually made up of a number of individual lines.

The **scan doubler** controls the quality of the image on the screen by doing exactly as it proclaims: doubling the number of lines of video, or creating the illusion of high-definition television (HDTV). When television was originally invented, it was designed as a moving system of interlaced horizontal lines. Video signals are limited to 525 horizontal lines of resolution. Whereas 525 lines is plenty for small television monitors, images projected onto large surfaces often reveal these individual lines. (The original TV inventors never saw a need for televisions to be bigger than nineteen inches!) The scan doubler literally doubles these lines, projecting 1,050 lines of resolution to the big screen. In addition to enhancing resolution, the scan doubler has controls for other quality adjustments such as color, hue, brightness, and sharpness. In general, do not be rash about adjusting the projector: it may be easier to tweak the doubler than the projector.

 Interlacing means that the lines are drawn on the screen in opposite intervals: odds, then evens. NTSC television is interlaced, whereas RGB computer displays are non-interlaced.

Techniques of switching

dissolves

Always look for an opportunity to avoid a sudden cut to an image during worship. Sudden movements when projected to a screen that is twenty feet tall can be abruptly disconcerting to worshipers. Most video mixers have mix options to allow a smooth transition between images. If you are operating without a mixer, try using black as a transition between various images.

fades

Another often used mixing feature is the fade. Though the goal of electronic media in worship is to keep the language spoken at all times, there may occasionally be a need to go to black. Common instances: brief transitions between elements of worship or while a speaker is praying. Or, the fader is a handy tool in covering mistakes! If the wrong image is projected, it is sometimes best to fade to black instead of showing several images while trying to get the right one on screen.

subtle stuff

The TD can help create a mood during live events by varying the transition times and using the auto take and auto fade buttons rather than performing these functions manually. For example, standard worship dissolves may be fifteen frames (half a second), whereas prayer dissolves or fade to black at the end of a message might be forty-five frames. These nuances will come naturally with experience, and distinguish a more experienced TD operator.

The TD can also assist the director and create a smoother, less intrusive flow for the images being projected. When the director gives the command to "take a source" (i.e., Take three), the TD should wait until the end of a sentence. Try not to switch from one camera shot to another, or from computer back to camera in the middle of a sentence, or when there is a lot of movement in the cameras.

Crew leaders/directors

The director is the decision maker for what happens on the screen during worship, and is the glue for any live media event. Some of the basic functions of the director role include:

- Gives commands to all other team members.
- Tells the technical director which source to project, based on the given scripts.
- Interacts with the "stage" director, who provides the congregational perspective and information about platform movement.
- Coaches the camera operators on establishing well-composed shots.
- Cues videotapes for projection, and plays them at the appropriate time (with some teams, it may make sense to allocate this function to someone else).

Because the director is the leader for the media team, it is important that he or she has at least a working knowledge of each of the pieces involved. Each role and each piece of equipment, has idiosyncrasies. An effective director will know what to ask, and what not to ask, depending on the capabilities of the equipment.

Anticipation

A good director anticipates like a chess player. The director must think ahead to the next few elements in the worship experience and communicate what is coming next to the team members. Time during transitions is critical during worship, which means that an unprepared team cannot react quickly enough to avoid the pitfall of the self-aware moment, when worshipers leave the state of worship and become aware of the technical process.

These moments of self–awareness precipitate the "production" complaint that Christian worship using electronic media is merely entertainment.

The production question is often posed to me concerning worship for the electronic media age. Those who ask this question, meaning largely established church leaders, have not made the distinction between the messages we are communicating and the medium in which we do it.

To date, the dominant messages of the electronic culture have been entertainment. As film marketers proclaim, let us entertain you, let us make you smile. As electronic media enters a stage of adolescence, however, we are beginning to see the medium spread to other areas of society. "Edutainment," or the use of video, graphics, and CD-ROMs in schools and universities, is the academic world's early acknowledgment that there is validity in the learning style of electronic media. Educators are realizing that electronic media precipitates a more fundamental shift in communication, which is at the base level of cultural interaction. Our thought processes are becoming different; we are no longer bound by the linear nature of the scientific method. "Meaning is found in experience" may be the best slogan for defining post-modernism. When a congregation is speaking this cultural language it is not entertaining. It is simply communicating the message of the Gospel in a way that concurs with how we now think, as products of our culture.

> Crisp, smooth navigation during the in-between moments of worship is key to the flow of a worship celebration. The congregation becomes unaware of the "production" behind the experience, just as the hearer of a powerful, moving sermon is unaware of the pauses and transitions in the preacher's voice. When the job is done right, all the attention is directed toward the experience of the "God-moment."

Multi-tasking

The director must be capable of multi-tasking, which means managing multiple strains of thought simultaneously. *Multi-tasking* is a computer industry term for doing multiple things at the same time. It is also called "stacking." The pace of our accelerated culture is such that the average person in our culture attempts multiple things simultaneously on a micro level, such as talking on the phone, writing a memo, and dealing with the person standing in the office. Even as the micro tasks are stacked, the same person is pursuing multiple agendas on a macro level, such as holding down a full-time job, attending school full-time, and starting a family. Most campus organizations have seen a dramatic decline in extracurricular attendance and participation because, unlike even ten years ago, most college students now attempt to hold down at least a twenty hour per week job while going to school full-time.

Multi-tasking is a part of the electronic culture, and a good director should master this non-linear system of thought or organization. During worship this means being cognizant of, literally, the Big Picture. What is happening at any given moment on the screen? The visual image is processed at a much quicker rate than is silent reading, or even listening. That means for worship there is never a dull moment. At each instant the screen must contain a relevant image, lest the "viewer" become distracted. Without even seeing a monitor, a preacher will know about a bad cue, because the lack of recognition is evident in the faces of the congregation.

Perceiving the big picture, then, means viewing the succession of images on the screen through the eyes of the worshiper. For media ministers raised in a literate, linear society, this is not easy to do, particularly during moments when the pace of images is quick, such as while directing a song or when incorporating graphics and video into a sermon. It is easy, as a reaction to the pressure of the live event, to forget for a moment what is happening on the screen. The results can be damaging. I have stories of moments in worship when the camera operator loses focus and we get a shot of a person's feet. In panic, the director spends far too long trying to figure out an alternative, and the shot stays on the screen long enough to ruin whatever momentum the speaker had built. The pace of this culture is instant. Call the shot first, before you have time to think about it. Effectiveness can sometimes be about trusting your instincts as a leader.

Keeping your cool

As goes the leader, so go the crew. The director must be able to respond to the unexpected with grace. Sometimes the speaker will forget or intentionally decide to skip a point or illustration, or give the improper cue. In that event, the director must reorganize and respond to the changes appropriately. For example, a director must decide on the spot if it is better to skip a graphic or bring it in late. Which will communicate the message to the congregation more clearly? Each service is different; with training and experience the right decisions will come.

Techniques of directing

Single versus multi-camera shoots

Video production approaches include single camera and multi-camera environments.

Multi-camera production is usually live, using different viewing angles to document the event as it happens. Single-camera, on the other hand, records all images to tape, which are then edited together to form a final product. Production is the process of recording images; post-production is the compilation and arrangement of the images to form a final product. For example, a live NFL football game is a multi-camera production; the feature on the star athlete that precedes the event is often a single camera segment, produced prior to the broadcast. You might use multiple cameras for worship, a live environment, but a single-camera for the produced video clips that are a part of worship.

Using more than one camera allows producers to capture the action from different angles and select certain shots through a switching device. It is important to alternate camera shots at appropriate moments. For example, do not switch to a camera shot when the speaker's back is toward that camera. It is better to stay with the selected shot until the speaker turns around, or choose another available option. In a multi-camera environment team communication is the key—everyone must be able to hear the director.

Shot selection

Have you ever watched a spectacular live event on television? Most of the world watches one every year, the Super Bowl. In the dramatic closing moments of a live sporting event such as this, viewers expect to be pointed in the direction of the action, and are liable to get upset when shown a shot of a kid in the bleachers, exactly as the fourth-down pass is thrown.

The director is responsible for this shot selection. In order to keep attention in worship on the event, rather than on the people producing it, the director makes every shot intentional. This means a constant toggling between the focus of the moment and other, supporting elements. These secondary shots are called cutaways.

A common example of the need for effective shot selection occurs in featured numbers during worship, which might be sung by the choir. An appropriate shot selection in such a case might be:

1. Opening medium shot of band
2. Medium shot of choir
3. Instrumentalist, finishing opening bars of the song
4. Singer, as begins singing
5. Second, different shot of singer, a bit tighter
6. Instrumentalist (brief)
7. Singer again

8. Choir, as begins singing
9. Singer, tight

In such a scenario, shots of the singer last longer, and cutaways of the band are shorter. If the choir begins a solo section or an instrumentalist a solo, then the focus of the song shifts from the singer. Always return to the action after one or two brief cutaways. Like any effective storytelling, the object is to build to a climax over the course of the story.

Be aware that there is meaning in various shots.

Alfred Hitchcock was a master at creating meaning in shot structure. In the film *North by Northwest*, there is a single shot that captures the essence of the film's story. As Cary Grant's character leaves the United Nations building upon realizing that he is being pursued for reasons he does not understand, his feeling of utter helplessness is perfectly captured by the extreme bird's-eye shot from atop the building. He looks like a little ant, and he feels like one, too.

Conversely, shots from underneath create a sense of power in the subject. Clint Eastwood's *The Man with No Name*, in Sergio Leone's spaghetti westerns, is often captured from underneath, with plenty of backlight. The large, silhouetted figure looks quite menacing.

Watch late–night television. At the end of most shows is a featured musical selection by a contemporary artist. Notice both the types and lengths of shots, and the shot selection by the director, and how these are ordered to communicate the feel of the action to the viewer.

Language

Like any new form of communication, electronic media has its own particular language, and this time I mean it literally. There are very specific buzzwords that media people need to know to communicate effectively, and it is important to teach these words throughout the ministry. (See the **APPENDIX** for command list.) In the heat of the moment, if a director has to call for an unplanned shot, it is a lot easier to say, "Take four" than it is to say, "Put the, you know, the—thing—up!" In addition, although it is best to work with static teams, for whatever reason there are times in which directors and/or team members must switch weekends. Universal jargon ensures proper communication, regardless of the team composition.

Timing

Timing is everything, and it is what separates a person who can hit the right button or call the right shot from the one who communicates a story through images. Pay close attention to subtle aspects of the service. When are short dissolves better, and when are long dissolves more appropriate? If your projector displays its input mode on the screen before the congregation, do you desire the moment in which switching the projector mode from "Video 1" to "RGB 1," which flashes those words on the screen, erases the work of the Holy Spirit in midair? Be aware of these little details, and strive to match the atmosphere being created by music, lighting, and the spoken word.

Anticipate cues before they come, so that graphics occur just prior to the cue, not with it or after. Always err on the front end of the cue. The same applies for videos. Always roll tape or cue the computer in such a way that the clip(s) begin as the speaker is finishing a sentence. Remember TV culture: How long is the black space between commercials and programming in broadcast television? The space between media elements should be short, as well.

It is also more pleasing to time dissolves so that they occur in tandem with live elements. For example, in a sermon, make camera transitions and graphic incues and outcues during breath pauses, rather than in the middle of a sentence, for smoothness, or less distraction.

Video clips

Depending on your technical configuration, video clips may be played off tape, through a computer, or directly from your computer's hard drive.

If the clip is on videotape, perhaps your video editor has placed a header prior to the clip for this purpose. Cue all tapes before worship!

Regardless, cue all clips at least two minutes before its scheduled airing in the sermon.

In order to prevent videotape stretching and ripping, a video deck usually has a safety feature that prevents it from remaining in pause mode for more than two minutes. Thus, if the introduction to the video piece is taking longer than expected, or if the tape was cued prematurely, the tape may be stopped or slightly adjusted while in pause mode to prevent it from stopping. Always be sure to recue tapes immediately after use for upcoming worship celebrations.

As learned in the school of hard knocks, when using a remote at any time during a live production, after use, set down the remote to avoid any inadvertent finger twitching that may cause the tape to stop.

Preparation for worship

Confirm with the entire crew every month, as part of your regular contact, the schedule for their service time. Be ready in case of emergency to help schedule someone else.

Use the checklist, (located in the **APPENDIX**), to ensure that all equipment, tapes, and graphics are properly prepared for worship. Sometimes equipment gets used for other purposes during the week, particularly in smaller and less established environments. Check to ensure that all equipment is configured properly and that switches are set to their proper position.

Review the order of worship scripts. Send scripts for worship ahead of time to directors via E-mail. There are two scripts:

Order of worship

One script is the order of worship, which is the same script handed to everyone involved with the worship celebration, from band members to dramatists, and sometimes to the congregation. It contains all the elements of worship, as well as dialogue for any pre-written elements, such as calls to worship, sacramental rituals, dramas, etc. This dialogue is an important cueing tool for the director.

Sermon script

The second document is the sermon script, which is a structured interpretation of the preacher's message, with cues and descriptions of media elements. The sermon script is created during the same weekday meeting that determines which graphics are made.

Meet with the speaker prior to the first worship to finalize the graphics and their cues. Often, incues and outcues change or graphics are moved or dropped depending on further sermon development. Have the speaker conduct a mock run-through of the sermon, hitting on every graphic or video illustration. During the run-through the director should listen along for unique ways that the speaker might indicate or cue a media piece.

Sometimes specific incues or outcues may not be listed on the sermon script. In this event, ask the speaker and make notes accordingly. As with all extemporaneous speaking, sometimes the preacher may adjust his or her sermon from what is written. In that event, the director must rely on knowledge of the sermon and key points the speaker might mention, as indicated in the script.

 Every speaker is different. Learn different styles of interacting with media elements.

Stay on your toes at all times; as with all live production, there is no telling what might happen!

Conduct the technical rehearsal along with the technical coordinator. The technical rehearsal is a mock-run of the entire service with all entities participating, and prevents your first worship event from being a run-through. A separate technical coordinator, who must integrate media with the other elements of the event, should run the meeting. This allows the director to focus entirely on the details of the big picture.

Make sure you project all graphics, including videos, text, and announcements during this time for confirmation or adjustment. It is common to encounter typographical errors or poor image quality during technical rehearsal.

Ask questions. The director is responsible for all content and transitions on the screen during worship. Again, pay particular note to transitions.

During the production, verbally state what events are ahead. Keep the entire crew aware of where the service is going. This keeps everyone in the loop and not merely a robot at your mercy. Function as a liaison with other team members, including the stage director and other media areas, to ensure that good communication is recurring. Feelings can be easily hurt during an intense production; most of the time this is through lack of communication. For unpaid team members, don't verbally disagree with a paid staff decision if there are other unpaid members present who could interpret this as dissension.

Spiritual leadership

On equal footing with the weekend celebration is the spiritual leadership that a director can provide. The media minister, paid or unpaid, is a pastor responsible for nurturing the presence of the Spirit in the lives of the team members.

Outside of worship, this nurturing involves many actions:

Make regular contact with all your team members, regardless of the degree of involvement or commitment. Ask accountability questions, such as, Are you reading for Bible study? Are you praying? Give them specific books that they can read and study. Answer spiritual questions if the need is present, and be available to recognize that need. How is their personal life? Are their relationships healthy? Do they tithe?

Find out if this is your team member's primary ministry. Are they serving regularly? If not, where else do they serve? And how often or how much? Help regulate that kind of activity, depending on the individual. For some, balance can be an issue; others could be exhorted to greater amounts of giving. Hold them accountable to service, not merely to technology.

Organize occasional events as suited to your team. Make some gatherings social and others based in spiritual growth. The emphasis on spiritual nurture in the media ministry team depends on church size (how many other types of small groups are providing this nurture?) and on the personal chemistry of the small group that is devoted to media ministry.

In team gatherings, interject often the spiritual impact of what we do: Cast vision. For example, point out persons in the congregation who are affected by what we do. Talk about the importance of ministry. Pray as a group prior to the event, for the specific purpose of the task at hand and also to encourage or develop awareness of the ministry as a place for transforming others' lives, and for personal transformation.

Do fun things with them. Take care of them in their service for instance by making sure food is available. Encourage them often while serving. Compliment their victories, and coach their defeats. When appropriate, take breaks from tasks at hand for fellowship.

For many in media ministry, this small group is their only means of accountability and transformation. Build for the future on this, their only training in the life of the body of Christ.

Exerting spiritual leadership during Production

When team members do not execute their task properly, which is an inevitable part of any live production, the director must be able to correct the team member in a Christlike way while ensuring that the task is completed well. This leader walks a tightrope between the poles of excellence and edification. Remember that each illustration or media piece may be critical to an unchurched person's understanding of the Gospel. To be excellent is to not "let something go" as "good enough," or to drop it from the production.

A tightly woven community of volunteers is one in which every team member realizes his or her contribution to the whole. This creates a sense of purpose that leads to finer production *and* fulfilled servants.

Furthermore, the director must be able to take charge of every situation over the headsets. Sometimes it is the tendency of team members to lose focus and begin chatting about irrelevant things. While occasional chatter may be good for building community, it should never interfere with the task at hand. It is the director's job to monitor its status, and to maintain the group's focus. When deciding what is an appropriate level of chatter, it is better to err on the side of silence.

Choosing a director and media ministry leaders

The proper understanding of the live production as part of the ministry is what separates the director from other ministry positions and from the secular media industries. The director is the hardest role to fill because the individual must have the technical expertise to execute the production and the compassion to do it with grace and encouragement. Either ability alone is dangerous; the former because the ministry will see a body count, the latter because the ministry will never achieve the level of excellence required to communicate the message effectively.

In mature media ministries, directors should be individually selected for apprenticeship. An apprentice will work one-on-one with a current director or media ministry leader for several live runs (months), learning every aspect of the position. Apprentices are evaluated by the current director, other directors on the team, and by the coordinating pastor during the training phase, to determine if and when the apprentice is ready to assume the leadership role.

If you are the first pastor or volunteer media minister at your church to attempt multisensory worship, it will be several months before it is possible to train an apprentice. Your training can come from the following sources:

1. Find another congregation in your region, where you can occasionally seek the help or advice of a willing mentor who is pursuing media ministry.
2. Attend a media ministry conference (such as the Media Reformation Conference, based in Ginghamsburg Church).
3. Take a course in videography at the local community college or technical institute.
4. Pursue long-distance learning over the Internet; for example, through trade magazine sites as listed in the Design section, which often have feature articles that cover use and application of technology.

Louis is a team member on the media ministry team in his church. He grew up at the church, and while a teenager had a number of negative experiences at church. While aware of Christ, his faith remained mostly intellectual, and perhaps wounded by the actions of others.

While in his twenties, Louis did not attend church often. But a few years ago, he returned and began to operate a camera once a month. Through the encouragement of directors in the ministry, he gradually began to take on more of a committed role in the ministry, serving not just once but entire weekends, often two times per month.

One summer the team invited him to become a director. Louis was hesitant, out of caution about the responsibilities, both in production and in spiritual leadership. But he accepted. Over the course of the summer he directed a number of weekends. The transition was not always smooth; one weekend the first service went so poorly that he wanted to quit out of frustration and feelings of inadequacy. But the media minister would not let him and he gained in skill and leadership as the months went by.

Beyond the technical requirements of the position, however, through the position Louis had begun to accept God's calling to spiritual leadership. He began a Bible study group in response to a need within the media ministry.

Louis is like the rest of us, a work in progress, growing into Christ's likeness. And it has been through involvement and eventually leadership in media ministry that he was transformed from a disillusioned teenager into a leader for the church.

The media ministry changes lives, and that is our objective.

---

1 Cordeiro, Wayne. "Building Church as a Team." New Hope Publishing: Honolulu, 1998. p. 120.
2 Ibid, p. 154.
3 "Bennis, Warren and Patricia Ward Biederman. *Organizing Genius: The Secrets of Creative Collaboration*. Addison Wesley, 1997.
4 "How to Solve Almost Anything," Diane Cyr. *Attaché*, November 97, pp. 46-49.

Part Four:
Buying the Tools

Ideas Drive Technology

"Every day 1.4 million presentations are made in the United States."

A friend asked me to help put together an entertainment center. It was one of those department store kits, with "some assembly required." It seemed to us that every piece was unassembled. It was an intense project and took a total of about fourteen person hours to complete. Most of the pieces of the furniture were joined by specialty screws housed in plastic casings. We felt fortunate that a mutual friend had donated his electric screwdriver for the occasion. However, approximately halfway through the project, the battery in the screwdriver died, and we didn't have a charger. So we gathered and used a motley collection of old-fashioned screwdrivers, the kind with a handle and one tip. Occasionally, I even used things not intended to be screwdrivers: a butter knife, a pair of scissors, a pocketknife. Somehow, we finished the project, and my friend is even proud enough to show it to guests.

Over the course of the project we used a number of tools of varying quality to accomplish the task at hand, and, except for the first time that we used the electric screwdriver, I don't think we once stopped to marvel at the tools we were using. The focus wasn't the tools. It was the project. Similarly, technology is neither the purpose nor the reason for media ministry, nor is it the most important aspect of the ministry. Don't confuse the means with the end.

Lessons on the Use of Technology

My experience with the entertainment center forms the basis for several lessons on using new media technology.

1. Don't let intimidating technology stop you from creating dynamic media.

Since the beginning of electronic media, inventive storytellers have used makeshift means to create other times and places. In the early 1960s, a teenage Steven Spielberg created a feature-length war film, using amazing special effects tools such as two by fours and mounds of dirt. His peer George Lucas made *Star Wars* on a low budget. Even as studios now spend incredible amounts of money on computerized special effects, and films like *Titanic* encourage behemoth production budgets, electronic media is becoming democratized. Entry-level workers in the entertainment industry have demonstrated the ability to create incredible stories with next to nothing of the available technology, such as entertainment worker Kevin Rubio who created the ten-minute parody "Troops." His *Star Wars* take-off was created entirely at home on his own Macintosh computer. I have even seen incredible storytelling from youth groups who were using nothing more than a VHS video camera, tape deck, and a four-track recorder.

Technology doesn't drive ideas. Ideas drive technology.

Why, then, you may ask, do Hollywood studios continue to spend so much? Because artists' dreams always outpace technology, and advances in technology encourage riskier creations. It's the same reason that futuristic visions of automatic kitchens turned into the reality of increased time spent cooking and cleaning. The law of accelerated culture is at work.

Jump in. Don't wait for the prices to come down or the technology to get easier. These are excuses that short-circuit the world from hearing the Gospel in an indigenous language. The time and resources required to make that happen are a part of doing ministry in the electronic age.

2. Don't let the tail wag the dog.

We almost gave up on the entertainment center when the screwdriver battery expired. It is at first devastating to lose your only good tool in the heat of the project. That was, until we began poking around and discovered a few old, beat-up tools that served the purpose. If one tool causes the shutdown of the entire project, the tail is wagging.

 I often read a media trade magazine. Trade journals are a good source for product reviews, technology updates, and creative applications.

Generally, they are required reading for anyone wishing to work in media, particularly in the professional vacuum that occurs while working in media in a congregation. The feature article in one issue proclaimed with huge, edgy type: "Content Is King!" That writer's epiphany may seem obvious, but he had simply fallen into the trap so common to technology users, the trap of putting electronic media technology before the messages that it is designed to send. Often, new technology is a solution without a problem. Make sure your purchases are driven by your vision, not the other way around.

Don't be like the fellow who likes to collect tools, who would show off his latest closet-sized red toolbox from the Sears catalog. Odd, though, that you never actually hear of or see him build something with those tools. Tools for him are about status: a real man possesses a loaded red toolbox, ready for any project, no matter how large. There is no point, though, in having highly specialized computers, plus video hardware and software, unless you have a clear idea of its intended use. Just like you never know what tools you'll need until you begin the project and read the manual, the types of equipment needed to begin a media ministry depend thoroughly on what it is that you want to accomplish.

So, if you've skipped straight to the technical section of this book, go back to the beginning and read the chapter on mission.

3. Technology is never state of the art, but it's never obsolete, either.

The entertainment center utilized a neat synthesis of old and new technology to fuse together its parts. Standard screws were housed in plastic casings, which could then be inserted into preset indentions in the wood. This enabled us to access the screws while the unit was partially assembled; yet it concealed them from view when it was done.

As with these inventive casings, electronic media is always a synthesis of old and new forms, both conceptually and pragmatically. Like other industries in North American culture, advancement in media is driven by technology, which is mandated by commerce. If we can now make something so good it will never break down, the best way to turn the crank of commerce is to create a new and better version of the same thing. This is why we continually see the latest and greatest quickly become the oldest and moldiest. (Of course, any experienced computer user can refute that newer is always better. When Microsoft upgraded its word processing application, Word, from version 5.1 to 6.0, it alienated many users by replacing their sleek, usable interface with a cumbersome, clunky interface that was so busy it left little room for composition and took up three times as much space on their hard drives. Internet chat groups sprang up denouncing the software and offering hints on how to keep the old version viable.)

interface: **means of interacting with a computer, conventionally through a monitor, or display**

Old does not necessarily mean obsolete. There are many ways in which older tools can retain their effectiveness.

While an intern at CBS Television City, Hollywood, I was amazed to see the original videotape technology still in use. The first videotape machines, wall-sized units that used videotape reels two inches thick and as large as a small automobile wheel, required extensive manual threading to operate. These ancient video machines were being used for a special archiving project in the basement of the facility! There are always uses for available technology. As the first wave of equipment purchases slowly get replaced with newer technologies, reassign the old to new uses: use it as a training device for youth, or as a mission project to enable work-program recipients to become literate in electronic media. Technology becomes synthesized with itself as it takes on new forms.

The fact that old stuff usually continues to work doesn't mean I fail to budget for new technologies. Although there are times in which technology is a solution without a problem, there are times in which the problems exist for a long time without a specific solution. As noted below, there still does not exist an ideal software application for integrating graphics into a live presentation. I have advocated Microsoft PowerPoint for several years, because of its ability to recognize multiple desktops for the purpose of separating thumbnails of images with a screen presenting them in full-view, in spite of the fact that PowerPoint does not have smooth, video-style transitions between graphics. Recently, a company called MetaCreations released a product entitled Kai's PowerShow, which does the opposite. It features smooth transitions between graphics, but only recognizes one desktop to do them on, and with an extremely odd interface to boot. So I continue as of this writing to search for the ideal application to present graphics.

Always opt for left–brained software interfaces for right–brained work. "Creative" interfaces simply interfere with the flow of ideas.

Thus, the media minister must constantly maintain the delicate balance of utilizing existing equipment while projecting future needs (and costs) against emerging technology. How difficult is that? New technology may be the media person's siren song. Extreme caution is urged, as there are *many* distracting toys.

4. Cost is a relative thing.

One of the first, and never-ending, things you may hear from a congregation that is contemplating electronic media is its insane cost. Professional video users tend to compound this perception by referring to the sort of equipment video production studios are purchasing, which tend to be upward of six figures annually. Further, this perception is compounded by early efforts of local churches in media ministry, which were invariably broadcast, and which is a terribly expensive venture.

Two principles apply: Advancements in technology are always initially expensive, and as more users purchase the technology and it mutates through various revisions, the cost of production drops dramatically. This is the law of supply and demand.

This is one of the greatest benefits of pursuing ministry in the language of the culture. Since most of the culture speaks the same language, cost per unit becomes inexpensive.

At one time, viewing a motion picture outside of a movie theater, which is the industry's established distribution system, meant contacting a non-theatrical distribution center, paying a licensing fee, waiting for the film in the mail, setting up a projectionist's booth at your facility, and so on. It was so difficult that it was rarely done. To see a clip from a feature film now, the cost and hassle are restricted to a TV, playback unit, and a videotape cassette or digital video disk. Most individuals already have two of these in their possession, and the third is available down the street for a few dollars. Furthermore, a computer with a tenth of the current processing power was at one time ten times as expensive as it is now.

Moore's Law (Gordon Moore, cofounder of Intel) has held true since 1967: "Computer processing power will double in size and speed every two years," and this pace has been good to consumers in the form of falling prices.

On the other hand, it is becoming increasingly expensive to speak a language that is no longer spoken by the majority of the culture. The cost of working in 8mm film has become very expensive in relation to videotape because it is so hard to find a processing facility, and maintain adequate projection equipment. (The Catholic church recognized a similar problem prior to Vatican II, when it was hard to attract new parishioners who were willing to listen to a shrinking number of Latin-speaking priests.)

As electronic media becomes digital, the lifetime cost of media hardware is becoming increasingly negligible. A home stereo system is analogous: phonographs needed replacement needles and cleaner for vinyl LPs, and cassette tape decks need their paths cleaned (often by a professional), but CD players require none of the above, as their primary operating device is a laser. Slide projectors require the weekly development of images into slide form, but computers can display an image for no additional cost (and its images are correctable, too).

Len's rule #5: The less expensive the tools, the harder you have to work to make them look and sound good, and the less likely that this will happen with amateur-level operators.

So, it does not take rocket scientists to produce media, and they don't need NASA's budget, either. Democratization of knowledge and technique is good. The B side to this, however, is that certain technological basics must be met in both the production and presentation of electronic media. These basics are outlined below in a series of steps, or phases. First, however, you will benefit from a short lesson on the tools of media.

Techno-Heaven

On the road, on the phone, and across cyberspace I have heard the same cry of "wolf" in various decibels: "Help! Only a professional can understand all these tools!"

 There has always been a close relationship between art and technology. For example, Renaissance artists were expert technicians at emerging technologies in paints, and at creating new paints to accomplish their creative visions.

Fear not. A few basic descriptions will enable you to make your way through trade magazines, which is the best way to increase your fluency and confidence. So, here are a few snappy answers to some good questions:

Video

What exactly is video?

Video is actually a series of still images that run past the eyes at the quick rate of thirty frames per second. Each still frame of video is composed of a number of horizontal lines, and the number of these lines is not to exceed 525, per national standards. Each of these thirty stills per image is actually composed of two *fields*, or half images, which occur sixty times per second, and are interlaced, like two hands doing the childhood imitation of "here's the church, here's the steeple."

 lines of resolution: **the number of lines that compose an NTSC signal. A rating unit for determining the quality of a signal.**

How do I acquire images?

In the early days, a complex system of tubes were used, but today the acquisition of images is a data transmission process in which images are converted from the lens of a camera to recordable information through a computer chip. Consumer-level cameras do this through a single composite chip (a one-chip camera). Industrial and broadcast cameras utilize three computer chips, one for each primary video color: red, green, and blue. The best video comes from three-chip cameras.

So, the number of chips determines the quality of video?

If it were merely up to the chips, all three-chip video would look as good as it does in the basement of CBS. But other technical variables have an impact. One variable is the aforementioned lines of resolution. Although 525 is the broadcast standard, the amount of lines of resolution in an image actually depends on the quality of the equipment. Though it is not the only barometer of a signal's quality, it is a good one. A typical industrial camera is capable of up to 740 lines of resolution, which is actually a huge number. But, the quality of a video image shrinks when forced onto analog videotape, which is capable of housing only a limited number of lines of resolution. (The process of recording video onto an analog tape requires another conversion, from digital back to analog, which results in the loss of some data. The better the tape, the less the loss. However, in the next few years, inexpensive digital video processing for editing and playback without the need for analog conversion will be making their way to consumers.) It's almost like squeezing everyone in the Bronx through the George Washington Bridge, on the way to New Jersey. The best tape format is when all the lanes are working (even though it is still a tight fit); the worst tape format is when they're doing construction on half the lanes during rush hour.

Lines of resolution	
Number of interlaced lines in a standard NTSC monitor	525
Number of lines in high-definition monitors	1,050
Number of lines a typical industrial camera can capture	740
Approximate number of lines in VHS videotape	250
Approximate number of lines in SVHS and Hi8 videotape	400
Approximate number of lines in Betacam and DV videotape	450

first generation: **The original video recordings. After an edit or dub, video on the dubbed tape becomes second generation, then third and so on. Third generation video and beyond becomes very difficult to work with, as the quality drops dramatically.**

Thus, the quality of first-generation video is only as strong as its weakest link, whether that is the quality of the camera, the videotape, or one of a number of other variables.

The wide world of cameras

Cameras range in quality from the little hand-held VHS-C camcorders found in consumer electronics stores to $250,000 broadcast studio cameras that never leave the cool confines of a basement studio. Basically, cameras fall into three categories: consumer, industrial (or corporate), and broadcast. In addition, there is a gray area between the first two, commonly called "prosumer." Although there are many technical differences among the categories, the obvious dividing line is price.

Comparable technical specifications in cameras include: the number of processing chips; the number of pixels that the computer chip(s) can process; the rating for low light conditions; and the signal-to-noise ratio, which is measured in dbs.

signal to noise: **the amount of pure video the camera captures in each frame versus the amount of spurious information, or noise, it captures)**

Explain the types of video formats to me.

The most popular videotape formats in recent years have included SVHS (a.k.a. Super-VHS), Hi8 (an enhanced 8mm videotape stock) and Betacam SP, which has been reserved for higher-end needs due to its expense, that being about four to five times as much as the previous two. Though there are many high-end post-production formats, Betacam SP has often been an industry standard for broadcast quality on location, or "in the field." For smaller production firms, including churches, Betacam SP has been too expensive, so other formats such as SVHS and Hi8 have been incorporated with success.

A new format is garnering attention, however, called digital video (DV). It matches the technical prowess of the best field analog format, Betacam SP, but costs no more than SVHS both in cameras and tape stock. Digital video at some point will replace analog videotape and be the standard for all video work, as it will carry the best quality signal at an inexpensive price and enable small organizations such as churches to do things that would have previously been cost prohibitive. DV, however, must first overcome industry squabbles, which have forced release and promotion of competing standards.

Once digital television (HDTV) becomes standard by 2005, the standards will cease to be an issue.

What is the difference between all the various video cables?

Check out the CD for images and descriptions of the primary connectors for video and audio.

There are really only three basic types of analog video cables. The most common is the composite cable, which contains the entire video signal and has either an RCA (like your home stereo and VCR) or BNC (round, metal, and latching) connector. Composite is the least expensive, lowest quality type of cable.

The second type, S-video cable, separates the video signal into luminance and chrominance, or brightness/contrast and color saturation/hue. The most common S-video connector is a weak four-pin plastic casing. The casing doesn't do a very good job of protecting the pins, which get damaged often. Another type of S-video connector is the Y-C, which is actually two BNC connectors split from a single cable, one for luminance (Y) and one for chrominance (C). S-video cable carries a better signal than composite because of its ability to separate luminance and chrominance.

The best-quality analog video signal is called component, which is a single signal that has been broken into a number of individual wires, each with its own BNC-style connector on the end. The parts are red, green, blue, vertical sync, and horizontal sync, with "sync" keeping the parts of the signal locked together. Component is the best-quality cable, as it separates each color into its individual spectrum and is able to maintain complete chromatic integrity.

The third type of cable is the RF cable, which is a complete video and audio signal. It is the same as the basic wire that most people receive from their local cable service, and is handy for wiring together multiple TVs/VCRs and monitoring workstations around a facility.

Lighting is way over my head.

The number-one rule about lighting: Make sure you have some. The number-two rule: Make sure there is more light in front of the subject than behind the subject. A basic attention to detail on light surroundings goes a long way toward professional quality video.

Inexpensive camera-mounted lights are available at many consumer video outlets. Professional field-production lighting kits can be purchased for about $1,000 and do a wonderful job of spreading even light across a subject. In the absence of a budget, however, it is possible to get away with such handy tools as shop worklights and incandescent lamps. Regardless of the type of light used, follow the basic three-part procedure, making sure that all light is the same color, as outlined in the Design and Team sections of this book.

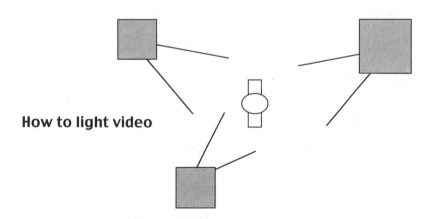

How to light video

Computers

Computers are a whole world in and of themselves, and the basics for getting around in a PC or Macintosh have become prerequisite for enacting media in ministry. Due to its complicated nature, the best method for learning about computers is through a separate publication, of which there are many on the market. Here I can answer a few questions regarding the graphics production aspect of computer technology.

The difference between a computer and TV is . . . ?

The images generated from computers and in video are inherently different. A computer signal is called an RGB signal, a technical anagram for the insider industry terms *Red, Green,* and *Blue.* RGB signals are non-interlaced, which means that the computer writes the screen line-by-line from top to bottom and then starts over again, many times per second. (In fact, the commonly quoted monitor rating, Hz, indicates how many times per second the computer writes the non-interlaced display. So a 75Hz monitor draws a full screen of lines seventy-five times every second.) Video, on the other hand, is in its final form an analog signal, and must conform to the guidelines set by the NTSC, or North American Standards Committee. (There are actually different standards for France and the rest of the world, called SECAM and PAL, respectively. As usual, we North Americans do things our own way!) Video is interlaced, as indicated above, so it draws its lines alternatively.

How do I get from one to the other?

Since the two signals are different, to be displayed together or in each other's realm, the computer signal must be converted to video, or vice versa. The most common method for presentation, converting a computer signal from non-interlaced to interlaced, is a process called scan conversion. "Scan converters" (little boxes with computer and video ins and outs), or video cards that accomplish the same function, are an indispensable part of any technical configuration involving both computers and video.

What about the other way, getting images *into* a computer?

There are three primary ways to place an image or series of images inside a computer, which is a process commonly known as "digitizing."

Flatbed scanners take a snapshot of a two-dimensional image, often a photograph, and reproduce the image within the computer. Scanning is the best means of digitizing flat materials such as slides and 35mm photographs.

Digital still cameras serve the same function as a traditional 35mm camera, without the need for film. Images are stored onto a small disk (compact or miniature), which can then be transferred into a computer system. Digital cameras are ideal for photographing three-dimensional objects for image manipulating and compositing.

Videotape from a video camera can be digitized into a computer through special video capture cards, most of which are expensive (though the price is dropping below $1,000), or through data transfer from digital video tape. In the near future digital video cameras will do to traditional cameras what digital still cameras are now doing to the 35mm still camera. At this point videotape will become obsolete as a means of acquisition, and everything will be processed with hard drives.

What is dpi, and why should I care?

"Dpi" is dots per inch, a term coined during print days to refer to the number of pixels, or little dots, that comprise an inch of ink on paper. Although dpi in the print world may be 150, or 300, or much higher for color reproduction, the highest dpi necessary for electronic images is 72. Anything more is wasted space.

pixel: the smallest unit of a digital display, and the name of my cat.

Further, the standard size for electronic images is 640 pixels wide by 480 pixels high, which conforms to the video industry ratio 4:3, as opposed to film's 16:9 ratio. This means that, unlike print, there are a maximum number of pixels in an image. When images are blown up to fit into a large screen, therefore, it may be possible to see the individual dots.

How do I show the completed images?

Images that have been digitized or created in the computer must be saved to a standard picture format and then placed into a presentation application for display. Some standard formats include TIFF, BMP (for PCs), and PICT (for Macintosh). Most presentation programs will accept these and other formats, and the best software applications are cross-platform, meaning files from them will work on both PC- and Macintosh-compatible computers.

How much RAM and hard-drive space do I need?

Video chews up hard-drive space. A typical two- or three-minute video production might take up 4GB of hard drive. The breakdown works like this: Uncompressed video is 600k/frame, or 18MB/second. Video compressed at a 2:1 ratio, then, is 9MB/second, and 4:1 video is 4.5MB/second. Most computer systems are capable of playing video at 4:1 compression; data at this rate, then, takes up 270 MB per minute, not including audio. As you can see, it adds up quickly, which means that video processing on a computer used for making media cannot also share space with the church management software program.

Graphics are no weenies, either: a typical worship service of fifteen to twenty graphics can easily take up 50 MB, which multiplied by fifty-two times in a year equals 2.6 GB. Removable storage and recordable CD-ROMs make good archiving mediums for storing data from crowded computer desktops.

This means that to facilitate all this data around your computer, you're going to need lots of memory. 80 MB is a good start; a powerful machine will have over 100MB. RAM is cheap and easy to get—and it is worth it, the first time you have a crash in the middle of a worship service or presentation.

Audio

How do I handle sound for my video clips?

Sound for movie and video clips should be routed through the facility sound system, particularly if the system is stereo. Most video decks have unbalanced audio outputs, which may be run directly to the soundboard. If video is sent through a video switcher, and that switcher has audio capability, then all audio-for-video signals should be routed through the switcher, and the switcher output routed to the soundboard. Then audio levels may then be monitored from the video board, with a static level established on the soundboard.

What about all the different kinds of microphones?

There are two basic types of microphones: condenser and dynamic. Condenser microphones take many forms, including wireless lavalieres, gooseneck microphones located behind some podiums, suspended microphones hanging from the ceiling for choirs and singing groups, and clipped microphones used to amplify instruments. Condensers require a power source, which may be corded or battery operated. Whereas instrumentalists prefer condenser microphones, dynamics are the favorite microphone of vocalists and some speakers. Dynamic microphones respond better to the inflections of the human voice (hence the word: dynamic) and reproduce low frequencies well. They are reliable, withstand a certain degree of punishment, and do not require a separate power source.

Microphones come in two basic coverage types, as well. Some microphones are omnidirectional, meaning they pick up noise patterns in a 360° circumference. Unidirectional microphones, on the other hand, are limited to a certain degree to angle of what occurs around the top, or diaphragm, of the microphone. Among unidirectional microphones, cardioid, supercardioid and hypercardioid all have certain advantages. The three have an increasingly narrower band of available space to pick up sound patterns. The ideal range for each of these microphones, defined as their "pick up angle," is defined in the following chart. Outside of the pickup angle, the output of the microphone is considerably lower.

Omnidirectional	360°
Cardioid	131°
Supercardioid	115°
Hypercardioid	105°

For more on audio amplification and reinforcement, purchase the *Yamaha Sound Reinforcement Handbook*, second edition, by Gary Davis and Ralph Jones, (Hal Leonard Publishing; www.halleonard.com) 1989.

Presentation

There are only 40,000 projectors to choose from . . .

The best way to understand the world of projectors is to break it down into feasible components. The first rating determines the brightness of a projector, or the ability it has to withstand ambient light. It is called the ANSI lumens rating. The higher the ANSI lumens number, the better the projector. Another important rating is the contrast ratio, or the difference that the projector makes between white and black. Again, higher is better.

ANSI lumens: **The rating unit to determine brightness output of a projector. The most popular technical specification for determining projector quality.**

Most affordable projection systems come in two popular digital flavors, LCD and DLP. Both are a single lens style. DLP, pioneered by Texas Instruments, is the newer of the two technologies and will eventually be better, although at present LCD is more ubiquitous and established. With either style, a minimum of 700 ANSI lumens is encouraged so that you can project an image without plunging the congregation into total darkness. Seven hundred lumens isn't an absolute figure, for there are other variables that defy general categorizations. For more information, consult industry trade magazines or web sites (such as www.computers.com) for periodic product reviews, which occur once or twice a year.

High-end (expensive) projection systems continue at this time to utilize the "three gun" technology, which is a separate lens for the red, green, and blue parts of the video signal. These CRT (Cathode Ray Tube) projectors are able to achieve higher ANSI lumen ratings and contrast ratios than digital projectors, and their price tag shows it. They continue to be the best available, as digital tries to replicate the density of data inherent in an analog system. However, they require more maintenance and have higher replacement costs than a digital projector. Their days maybe numbered as digital technology improves. Their advantage, however, is also in their age. Being analog units, they are able to reproduce video with finer detail than LCD and DLP projectors—an important distinction when speaking to a TV culture, and not a computer culture.

Low-maintenance equipment is equally as important as quality. If the best quality requires an engineer to operate, and no engineers are around, then it won't stay that way for long. Ditto if the best quality requires regular, expensive visits from the dealer's service department. There is little purpose to owning the most expensive piece of equipment, if it can never maintain its original state. Some projectors may fall under this category: improperly converged or configured, you may end up with little green people. Whether it is buying a plug-n-play projector, or setting up permanent cameras, do whatever is necessary to avoid needing the services of an engineer every Saturday and/or Sunday.

The most important thing to remember about projection screen quality is the role of ambient light in a room. The best image in the world cannot withstand the direct assault of light. Why do you suppose movie theaters are dark? Focused light directed to places on the front platform removes direct light from screens and allows even mediocre projectors to look fairly decent.

How big a screen do I need, and what kind?

There is actually a rule for determining the best screen

size for a particular space. Formulated by SMPTE, or the Society of Motion Picture and Television Engineers, the rule is called the 2x6 rule: the screen width should equal the distance in feet to the first row of seats, divided by two, and equal the distance to the last row of seats divided by six. In case the two are not the same, go with the larger figure. Screen height is then adjusted proportionally, adhering to the 4:3 ratio that is television. This means that a typical twentieth-century church sanctuary (less than fifty years old) would need at least a twelve-foot-wide screen for a congregation of five hundred.

As to what kind, there is a difference between front and rear screens, as opposed to projection systems. Front screens are matte white, usually a reflective vinyl surface, whereas rear screens may be composed of vinyl, acrylic, or even glass that is non-reflective. Rear screens cost a bit more, but hide the projector, which is better aesthetically. Since nearly all sanctuaries, built in the pre-electronic era, are designed to allow natural illumination, rear screens deal with ambient light better. On the other hand, unless you cover up the organ pipes or choir box, few sanctuaries have the extra room to allow for a rear-mounted projector. In this case, shutters or other options that convert light from natural to artificial might give you the ability to direct light away from the screen.

As far as number of screens, this depends on the physical space. Some rooms are so long and narrow that multiple screens are crucial for proper viewing. But if possible, stick with one large screen. It keeps the congregation focused on the activity at hand, and in the line of sight for sermon graphics, while avoiding the "tennis match" effect of having to look at either the speaker *or* the graphic.

How can I hook together several TVs?

The best way to attach multiple monitors to a single source is through a routing device. The simplest router is an RF splitter, which splits a single RF signal into a number of signals. Although RF cable will maintain signal quality for up to one hundred or more feet, other kinds of video cable tend to lose signal quality. Hence the need for a device that can boost the signal as well as distribute it. Such devices are called Distribution Amplifiers, or DAs. It is wise to boost any split signal into multiple outputs. Don't ever "Y" or "T" a signal without amplification, as the signal simply splits into two halves, both being too weak. Also, RF signal that will run across long stretches of cables (over one hundred feet) will need to be split through a DA, because the signal begins to degrade.

Tape duplication

Should we record worship services for distribution on audiocassette?

Audiocassettes serve a very useful ministry purpose, for both the community of believers at a local church and throughout the church universal. It is well documented that retention rates from oral presentations are pathetic in our electronic culture. Beyond the addition of electronic media as a part of the presentation, audiocassette copies provide a valuable tool for reinforcing core messages. They have a powerful dual impact when combined with memory or description of tangible, visual metaphors. Not only do they enrich, educate, and promote spiritual growth, but audio-cassettes can also be a handy evangelism tool for the work-place and to people in other geographic areas, which is of increasing importance in our a-physical, Internet world.

Okay, what duplication process should I use?

Although there are other, possibly higher-quality meth-ods, the least expensive method to duplicate an audiocas-sette is through special duplicating machines. A number of companies sell audio duplicating machines that may be operated independently or hooked together. In the latter case the master is placed on one machine, and the others read from it as "slaves."

For more information, consult tape specialists such as Kingdom Cassettes Ministries at P.O. Box 506, Mansfield, PA 16933, 800-788-1122, www.kingdom.com.

Other important stuff

Where can I find out more about the world of electronic media?

There are a number of trade magazines available free to media professionals (read: money spenders) in order to keep up with the changing technology. Trades are helpful for becoming acclimated to the world of electronic media, staying up on emerging technology, and as a resource for companies offering media products and services. I first began learning about electronic media through the world of trade magazines. Some include:

- *NewMedia* magazine, 800-253-6641, www.newmedia.com The longest running multimedia trade publication; available free

- *Digital Video* magazine, 888-776-7002, www.dv.com Subscription fee, but worth it—a number of helpful product reviews and user tips in every issue

- *Presentations* magazine, 800-328-4329, www.presentations.com Free trade publication aimed at the business market; contains many helpful techniques on the integration of media into presentations; useful for educators

- *Video Systems*, 913-341-1300, www.videosystems.com Free trade publication; official publication of (ITVA) International Television Association; good product reviews and industry contact information

- *AV Video and Multimedia Producer,* 800-800-5474, www.kipinet.com/av_mmp/ Free trade publication aimed at the non-Hollywood production and post-production industry. Articles on location shoots helpful, as well as product reviews, etc.

In addition, a number of computer trade magazines such as *MacWorld* and *PCWorld* frequently cover media-related issues.

The Phasing Plan

Why should I phase?

You may find that the best way to implement media technology into church life is through a series of purchasing phases, over a planned length of time; for example, one phase per six months or year. Why phases? As opposed to one large purchase, phases may be appropriate to your situation for a number of reasons:

Cost involved

Most churches that begin media ministry don't have the luxury of incorporating it into a new facility but rather must integrate it into an existing environment that is not user-friendly. The unfriendly space often precludes a capital budget, which forces leaders to cast a vision for every penny. An initial phase or two may not only be cost-effective, but may lead to easier vision casting, which in turn will lead to more funds for additional phases.

Acceptance over time

The second most stated comment from visitors experiencing media in worship for the first time, after expressing awe at the experience, is that it is a major production. Any foreign structure is always obvious on initial contact, and the same is true for worship production. Although every form of worship is a form of production, from High Mass to campfire singing, most worshipers are oblivious to the form because it has become an intimate part of their experience. The best way to adapt a congregation to a new form is to introduce it in small enough increments that it is easily accepted.

A church in Oregon did this in such a way that the drive for media in worship became a process of responding to the congregation. The worship leader would show a movie clip one week, wait a few weeks for the furor to die down, show another, wait a few more weeks, and so on. Eventually the leader began to hear requests for more film clips and electronic media. Instead of fighting a theological battle with the congregation over worship forms, this worship leader planted seeds and quenched the thirst. Instead of a teeth-pulling, top-down experience, the media ministry became a grass-roots church movement.

Evolving ideas for use

Refer to Part One on literacy. Once a church has been producing media for a while, it will begin to understand what sort of stories and messages can communicate best.

Capitalizing on these styles may dictate additional purchases. It is best initially not to purchase tools without knowing their potential use, lest they end up collecting dust. Again, ideas drive technology.

Phase 1: Showing pre-produced video
What you get

Pre-produced video allows you the ability to show high-quality films to illustrate and interpret messages in a visual context. Films can do what other media forms cannot. A few years ago, I showed a clip from the film *Rudy* in a worship service on the theme of perseverance. *Rudy* is the tale of an undersized young man who through sheer will earns his place on a Notre Dame football team. The clip brought grown men to weeping. Manipulative? Maybe. I call it speaking in a language that people understand. (It's not any more manipulative to make people laugh with well-timed humor; the stigma is associated with crying.) Electronic media, particularly video, is an inherently persuasive language tool. Video and graphics persuade through an appeal to senses, through an interpretation of the image, rather than through linear, analytical reasoning skills. This communication moves past head knowledge to the place where people's hearts become, as John Wesley once said so eloquently, "strangely warmed." Messages that speak in these ways are messages remembered long after their delivery. I don't remember much about the words or sentence structure of that sermon, but the *Rudy* clip inspires me to recall spiritual truth contained in that sermon, to persevere. As a dynamic contemporary metaphor that connects with my physical leisure, it "updates" the athletic imagery that the apostle Paul used for running a race or putting on the full armor of faith. A properly selected film clip, used with discretion (and without violating copyright), can accomplish the same thing for your message.

What you need

- An existing TV and VCR (every church has one on hand, at home or at the office; if not, you may have more of a daunting task than I am leading you to believe), with an RF cable between them

- A film license
- A nearby video store

What it costs

- $100

Licenses are inexpensive. Refer to the Appendix for a more complete look at the copyright question.

Phase 2: Display
What you get

More than half of the congregations in North America have fewer than thirty persons in a given worship service. For this size, one 25" TV will do. But if your space is larger than that, it is necessary to set up a means by which everyone is close enough to a monitor.

What you need

There are basically two options.

- NTSC video projector, minimum of 700 ANSI lumens with SVHS, RCA, and RGB ins and outs (I/O)

- Large projection screen

- Cart to put it on, a power strip and/or extension cord, and a set of RCA cables to run between the VCR and projector

One option, the most commonly assumed, is to purchase a centrally located projector with a screen large enough to satisfy everyone, even the back row. Usually, in the context of the mid-twentieth-century rectangular worship spaces, this means a very large projector. Be aware that the quality of a projector, unlike televisions, is dependent on the amount of ambient light surrounding it.

Four easy steps to purchasing a projection system:

1. Find at least two trade magazine articles on projection systems.

Don't let the rapidly changing nature of electronic media deter you from making a purchase. The shelf life of a unit is long enough to justify its expense. Remember that although nothing is really state of the art, it takes a very long time for a unit to become truly obsolete.

2. Notice the few primary differences between the units, and mark these categories, with notes on each unit (See above on projector specifications).

3. Determine which categories speak best to your needs. For example, do you just need a video projector, or one with data input as well?

4. Have three local vendors bring units to your facility and show you what they look like in action. (The units are expensive enough that this shouldn't be a problem.) Try to convince the vendor to lend you a unit for a weekend service, to view it in its context. Make sure to have some content, for which you'll need a projector!

In addition to or instead of a projector, another option:

- Four more TVs (27" screen)

- RF cables. Make them at least 25' long, or long enough to reach from TV to TV.

- Stands or carts for each television

- Coaxial splitter (available at most electronics stores, for splitting the RF signal into four signals to route to the televisions)

Instead of one large screen, the second possibility is to set up multiple small screens throughout the worship space. A good rule of thumb is that a 27" television properly placed will service the viewing needs of fifty people. Thus, if the worship space is small enough for two-hundred people or less, it may make more money sense to go with four 27" televisions, acting as monitors, on mounts or carts. These might be positioned as one in front on each side of the front of the worship space and one each along the side aisle halfway back. Another option, for mid-sized congregations with long worship spaces, is to configure a combination of both options, with a projector in front and TVs in the rear.

What it costs

• $1,500 for TVs, $10,000 for projection

Entry-level projection systems run as low as $4,000, but one that fits the needs of most sanctuaries retails for approximately $10,000. Televisions, on the other hand, can be as low as $250 for a 27" screen. On the latter count on accessories to cost $100 per television.

Phase 3: Computer technology
What you get

Computers open up a world of graphic possibility and are the major step in realizing a church's potential to make media ministry integral to church life. Potential uses are boundless:

• Song lyrics can be projected onto a screen, allowing congregational singing to live up to its name, instead of being an isolating experience in which worshipers stick their noses in hymnbooks.

• Scriptures can be projected, providing a hospitality function for people who didn't grow up in the culture of carrying leather Bibles on Sundays.

• Sermon points on a screen keep worshipers focused, and maybe the preacher, too.

Most importantly the foundation has been set for the creation of original visual images, which is the key to interpretive electronic media. As noted, at the simplest level computers are capable of doing what was formerly the domain of slides and overheads. Although the initial cost outlay is greater, computers are self-contained units, not needing weekly production expenditures, as with the older technologies. In addition, a computer is uniquely able to accommodate the last-minute whims of worship leaders.

What you need

- Any PC- or Macintosh-compatible computer system with at least 150 MHz processing power, RGB output, a CD-ROM, and a removable storage drive

- A 17" monitor with the ability to display at least thousands of colors, (15" monitors, although not preferred, will suffice)

- <u>At least</u> 64 MB RAM and 2 GB storage space

- Presentation software such as Microsoft PowerPoint

- Either a video/accelerator card or a scan converter

There are many ways in which a computer can interface with a VCR and TVs or projection. Outlined are four possibilities, on a scale of least expensive/quality to most expensive/quality, excepting the fourth option, which is high quality at a low rate, with one major caveat.

Option 1: Scan converter

Summary: The RGB (monitor) output of the computer plugs into the scan converter, and the scan converter plugs into the line input in the VCR via video cable (RCA or SVHS). VCR line output is then sent to the projection or monitor display. Scan converters work with a one-monitor system, or one "desktop." While presenting, there is no way to check the order of graphics on a separate computer display. Some signal from the computer is lost in the transfer, but it is an inexpensive and easy way to mix computer graphics and video clips seamlessly into a presentation.

Diagram 4.1

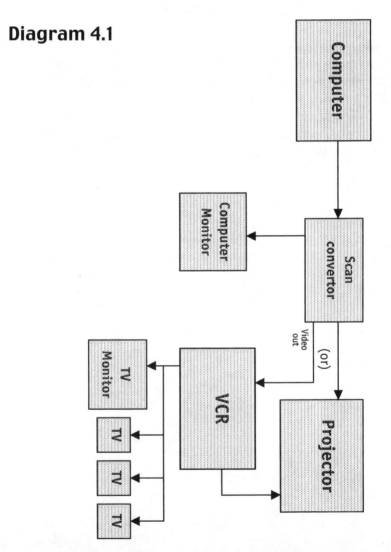

Option 2: Video card, post VCR

Videos run from the VCR into the computer through the video card line input, allowing an RGB (computer) signal to plug directly into a projector. This increases signal quality while eliminating the need for multiple inputs on a projector, and the subsequent dreaded mode shifting during worship. (Transitions during a service are crucial moments.) It also houses two monitor displays, giving the user the option to see individual graphics while in presentation mode. Option 2 is slightly more expensive but the best option barring further expansion. However, RGB signals are sometimes brutal on video signals, killing the chrominance.

Diagram 4.2

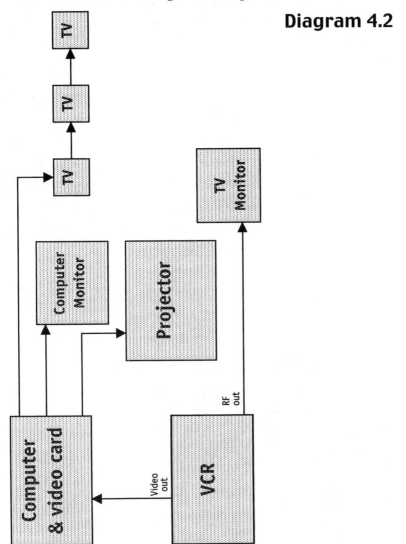

Option 3: Video card, pre–VCR

The computer output is sent via video cable (RCA or SVHS) into the line input of the VCR, then to display. Like option 1, except replacing an external scan conversion card with an internal video card, creating two monitor displays. Better quality, slightly more expensive. The best option for further expansion to video mixing with live cameras.)

Diagram 4.3

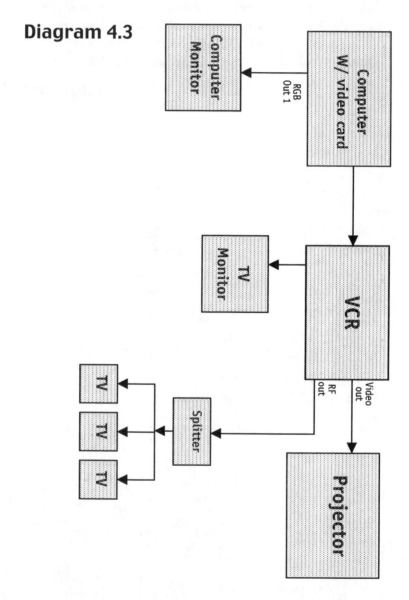

Option 4: Neither

Most projectors have separate RGB (computer) and RCA/SVHS (video) inputs, eliminating the need for conversion to video. Like option 1, this is a one-monitor configuration. This option will create the best inherent computer signal, but forces the user to toggle between computer and video mode in worship. Toggling is horrible, as it disrupts the flow of worship by creating the dreaded "self-aware" moment exactly as transitions are to carry the worshiper between worship elements. Least expensive, this option is best for computer display only, but worst for mixing video and computers, and only allows for the use of televisions via output from the projection, which is not a feature of all projection models.

Diagram 4.4

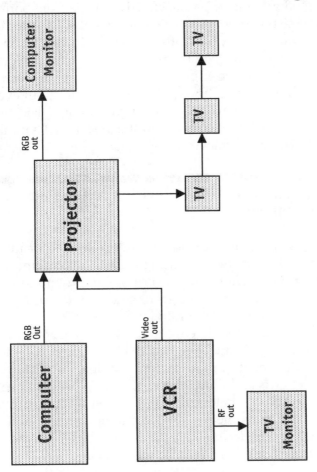

What it costs

$3,000

A good computer system, outfitted as above, will cost approximately $1,500, not including software. Scan converters range from $150 to 500, but avoid the cheap ones, for the quality *really* begins to suffer. Video cards are $250 and up, and must include both an RGB out, which is advertised as an accelerator, and video ins and outs.

Phase 4: Original graphics

What you get

The means to design and produce the graphic images detailed in Part Two and in the CD-ROM. Creatively designed graphics separate effective media from boring business-style presentations composed of solid-color gradients and opaque, fully offset drop shadows. The objective is not to create computer effects. Strive for a television look rather than a computer look. Approximately one-half of North Americans have personal computers, but everyone has a television, and they watch a lot of it! The television is the look they expect and the look a media ministry should strive to achieve.

Make your media like television culture, not computer culture.

Original graphics bring a higher potential for interpretation. Instead of repeating the text of a Scripture reading on screen during a sermon, an illustration, either original or derived from stock photography, can persuade using post-literate language.

Good models for effective graphics come from cable networks. Sports channels such as ESPN, or programming and station identification on networks like the History Channel, Arts and Entertainment, and CNN epitomize television graphics—bold, colorful, with depth. Strive for these styles, and along the way utilize photography, stock and your own, with frames, edges, and montages. See the design section in Part Two for more details.

What you need

- Image manipulation software. Adobe Photoshop is the standard, but other tools might suffice.

- Photoshop plug-ins, or add-in features, aren't necessary but very helpful for those occasions when pressed for time.

- A thirty-bit color flatbed scanner and/or a digital camera for image capturing.

- Removable storage capability for transfer and archiving.

For non-artists, or beginning graphic artists, there are many ways to accelerate your learning curve. A variety of sources offer pre-produced images and art for a small fee. Some companies include:

- Artville, (800) 631-7808, www.artville.com

- Corel Image Library, (800) 772-6735, www.corel.com

- Cyberphotos, (800) 990-DISC, www.cyberphoto.com

- ImageClub, (800) 661-9410, www.imageclub.com

- PhotoDisc, (800) 528-3475, www.photodisc.com

- Publisher's Toolbox, (800) 390-0461

Software:

Adobe Corporation, www.adobe.com
Illustrator (vector drawing program)
PhotoShop (2-D graphics/ image manipulation)
After Effects (video layering/compositing)
Premiere (video editing software)

Microsoft Corporation, www.microsoft.com
Microsoft Powerpoint (presentation)

MetaCreations, www.metacreations.com
Kai's PowerShow (presentation)
Painter (2-D graphics/ image manipulation)
Expression (vector drawing program)
A number of 3-D products including: Bryce, Painter
3-D, Infini-D, Poser, Ray Dream Studio
Final Effects (plug-ins for Premiere, After Effects)

What it costs

$1,600

There's no limit to the amount of money one can spend on software, with all the extras that are on the market. Count on spending at least $600 to $800 to get started. Basic image acquisition hardware, whether scanner or camera, should cost $800, though prices rapidly fall on cameras. Be careful with $49 scanners that may be junk. Scanners are best for flat images, like photographs, whereas digital cameras are best for any three-dimensional object, like a bottle, car, or building. Removable storage is as little as $90 for drives, and $15 each for cartridges.

Phase 5: Original video

What you get

The power of the creative juice gushing from your teams will eventually overtake the technical hurdle of creating original video. Video opens up a world of potential to a worship or teaching experience. Testimonies edited to two minutes, with background music and environment shots, can tell a story much more powerfully than a twenty-minute microphone exposition. Montages can create a mood to match a message in drama, music, or the spoken word. Brief visual narratives, of the sort found in contemporary commercials, can set up the metaphor for an event. With digital technology, there are fewer limits to the creative mind.

What you need

A means of acquiring video with audio:

- Industrial level three-chip DV, SVHS, Hi8, or Betacam format camcorder

- Professional audio (XLR) input adapter, depending on the camera (some cameras have this feature built in)

- Clip-on and dynamic microphones and supporting XLR cables

- Camera-mounted light(s) and/or a field lighting kit

A means of editing video:

The presence of computer technology has overturned conventional wisdom on video editing. As opposed to old paradigms for compositing video, it is now possible to edit in a non-linear fashion. The transition is analogous to the move from typewriters to word processors. A typeset word could only be changed with a bottle or 1x3 paper slip or whiteout, and its physical proximity on a page was permanent. Similarly, linear video editing is the ordered sequence of shots applied to videotape, and reordering of the sequence required a completely new edit. Word processing has allowed users to figuratively cut and paste sections of a document, composing and ordering thoughts in a non-linear fashion or method that matches the creative process of most persons. Non-linear video is the visual equivalent, a process that frees the mind to concentrate on the narrative as opposed to its construction. These advances are making it possible for amateurs to create incredible video. It is the democratization of media.

Early non-linear digital video editing schemes (NLE, to industry insiders) were extremely expensive, costing buyers $50,000 and more to convert analog video to the digital realm and back again. Newer versions feature a much lower price point, which is still expensive compared to what is possible with DV format video. With DV, it is possible for a computer to retrieve video data directly from the digitally encoded tape, eliminating the need for an input deck and saving a generation in the process. This means that a user only needs the right kind of computer, a video monitor, and software to create incredible video.

Another possible need during the post-production process is stock music. Stock (or "buy-out") music is composition created for the purpose of accompanying video. Arrangements can be made with clearinghouses to purchase CDs of stock music, which come with a copyright clearance for usage. Prices may range from $40 per CD to thousands for a library. (See Part Two, page 59.)

- Macintosh- or PC-compatible professional model mini-tower computer with monitor, at least 100 MB of RAM, over 200 MHz processing speed and a 17" display or larger

- As much storage space as you can afford, at least 8 GB

- 19" video monitor (a big TV with 5-video input will suffice)

- Video capture card (for retrieving digital video in and out)

- Over-the-shelf editing software such as Adobe Premiere 5.0 or proprietary software such as Avid or Media 100 (the latter of which also includes the necessary hardware)

- Stock music CDs

A means of presenting the video

Basically, there are two ways to present videos created in the digital realm: remain in the digital realm, or "dump" to tape. "Dumping" is the process of mastering a video from the editing system to videotape for playback in a traditional videotape deck. For ease of use in the course of a tense live presentation, videotape playback remains, for the time being, the smoothest alternative. In addition, most computer systems are still not yet capable of playing back a full-motion, full-screen video from a computer system. As this changes, video playback will become easier from a computer than from tape, and ultimately better quality as well (refer to the 250 lines of VHS resolution!).

full motion = 30 frames per second; full screen is 640–x480, as opposed to postage–stamp-size video characteristic of early multimedia

- SVHS, Hi8, or Betacam videotape deck(s) for playback, two being important to mix multiple video signals together concurrently, or back-to-back

- Remote controller for playback during presentation

What it costs

For the whole job, at least $14,000

- A video camera for image acquisition. A mid-range DV format camera does a wonderful job, and only requires a small adapter to receive professional audio input, $5,000.

- Audio for video, including a cartioid and a dynamic microphone and audio cables, $800.

- A camera mounted light, $200.

- An entry-level non-linear video editing system, with software and third-party boards, currently tallies at $5,000, though prices frequently change.

- SVHS deck for playback, $2,500. Stock music and video-tape, $500.

While it is not possible to pay for a video system with coffee money, consider that $14,000 for an editing system, spread out over three years, is $389/month, which is about the same per month as the cost of one weekend projector, camera, or computer rental. Further, compared to the at least $150/hour rate charged at most post-production studios for editing time, a system is paid for with the production of ten video clips. You may find that ten clips are produced very quickly with such a system.

Phase 6: Cameras

What you get

Live switching is the most expensive of all the phases, but the most necessary for large congregations. In a congregation of more than one-thousand, there cannot be one-thousand good seats, but unlike theater managers, church leaders are gravely concerned that the people in the rear have an experience equally as good as those in front. This means bringing the activities of the platform to where they are.

In addition, the presence of live cameras can enhance the meaning of a live event, as discussed in the section on directing (page 101). The experience of a piece of music becomes more complete for the worshiper in the electronic culture when confronted by a visual interpretation of the song, whether that is a narrative form or a re-creation of the performance for a visual context. Sermon retention rates rise with the addition of visual listening forms to accompany oral presentation.

What you need

There are actually two hardware considerations to this phase. The first is the addition of the video switcher or mixer. This device coordinates the various signals, provides a means to switch or toggle between them, and sends them out to a common output. Mixers also contain a variety of wipe and dissolve options, and many feature "keying" ability. TV weathermen use one type of keying, chroma, to give the weather forecast over computerized maps (another type of keying, luminance or luma key, is popular in video post-production). Most broadcast facilities use large switchers containing sixteen or more inputs; live events for the life of the church will suffice with approximately eight options.

"Keying" a color removes it from the video signal and overlays the signal onto another video signal.

The second hardware consideration is the cameras themselves. Live cameras are the final, most professional stage of managing a media ministry, and require the most from the teams of volunteers involved. This doesn't mean six-figure studio cameras, necessarily; industrial-level studio cameras will suffice, with proper installation and a good mixing console to integrate the variety of live, computerized, and video sources. Here is one possible configuration, based on a two-camera setup:

Diagram 4.5

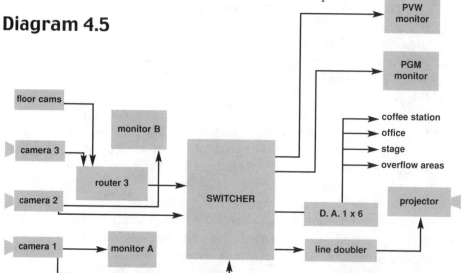

What it costs

- Two or three industrial quality studio cameras, $7,000/each
- Support equipment for cameras (pedestals, camera controls, AC), $2,500 apiece
- Video cables, $1,000
- Video mixing console with Time Base Correction, $4,000
- Monitors for multiple sources, 5 @$400 each=$2,000

The final configuration

With everything combined, a final media schematic might look like this:

Diagram 4.6

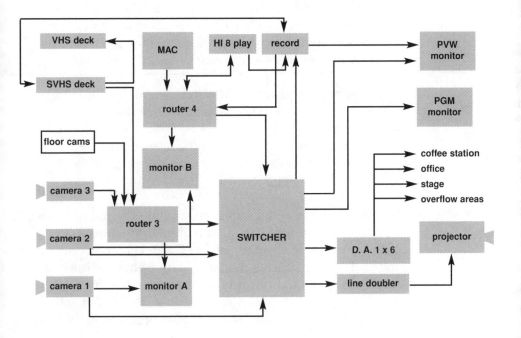

All the phases together add up to a big bill, but do not forget the primary purpose for pursuing media ministry. Communication is not about budgets but about changing lives. One church in Pennsylvania, averaging 600 a weekend during two Sunday morning services, began a media-driven worship service based on a seven-team structure of hospitality, drama, computer graphics, video, audio/lighting, music and resource/worship planning. The service was targeted to the unchurched of the local community. By its tenth week, the new service was up to 150, raising the church's weekend population by 25%.

A church in Connecticut has reversed long-term decline through the use of media. The pastor told me, "worship attendance is up 13 percent in the past year. Given our recent history, even a zero would be a plus." Saying that the use of media has generated excitement equivalent to a new church start, the pastor has witnessed a dramatic increase in mission involvement and giving. Further, many new young families and faces have begun to pepper a traditionally aged crowd on Sunday mornings. He anticipates a second worship service to begin in the fall.

A young college graduate at a state school in Ohio began advertising for a campus media ministry startup. His response was too great because he did not have the systems in place to handle the significant response he received. He had to turn away scores of eager people while he left campus to raising funding and facilities.

These are stories of life brought about by the use of media in ministry. The daily detail of a ministry that uses electronic media to communicate the Gospel is time-consuming and not without its struggles, but ultimately it is worth the pain and toil, as churches grow and lives are transformed into the likeness of Christ. This is the goal and desire of any ministry conducted in the name of Jesus Christ.

Appendixes

The Media Ministry Job Functions

When hiring a media minister, or when guiding one or more volunteers in media ministry, you should look for enough of the following skills to make a match with your church. The elements of the description below, when taken as a whole, suggest a large church structure. If your church is smaller, edit the description.

Creative

- Visionary: Demonstrate necessity of media in church life through excellence in production.

- Planner: Oversee electronic media content for church life, including weekly worship celebrations, education needs, church life campaigns, and broadcast advertisements.

- Advocate: Promote visual thinking in program development in all areas of church life.

- Storyteller: Compose the thoughts and visual images that will form a coherent visual story.

- Theologian: Critically evaluate the interpretive power of the visual medium, making sure to preserve the integrity of the Gospel.

- Producer: Develop scripts, draw storyboards, and plan integration of graphics and music for video features; create graphic looks for worship and education series.

- Coach: Guide media assistants in electronic media design, for 2-D, 3-D, and video.

- Continuous learner: Stay current with cultural trends in media content by watching television, film, and 2-D mass media (advertising, periodicals, etc.).

Administrative

- Oversee all budgeting for media ministry.
- Lead all coordination of scheduling for live and production needs for worship and educational media.
- Evaluate and approve all media purchasing, from capital equipment to production needs to ongoing materials.
- Archive all media content in database form.
- Design structures for new ministry components of media, such as media content and presentation for education.
- Evaluate and determine staffing and personnel needs for media ministry.
- Determine best service arrangements for equipment maintenance, oversee all equipment upkeep.
- Promote the needs of the media ministry in church life.

Relationship

- Develop leadership within the media ministry, including (at least) weekly conversations beyond technical/administrative issues with team leaders in video, sound, lighting, and tape.
- Host monthly small group meetings within the media ministry and direct social and spiritual gatherings for the ministry as a whole.
- Recruit new members into the media ministry while developing fringe participants.
- Train team members of the media ministry in relevant technical areas.
- Impart spiritual leadership and wholeness to the teams and people of the media ministry.
- Create environments where people feel part of a community.
- Provide accountability and developmental guidance for media staff teams professionally and spiritually.
- As possible, develop relationships with other media ministry professionals throughout church and with secular media industry professionals.

Technical/Production

- Oversee operation of in-house computer systems, all computer systems related to education/presentation, all production and live video operations, and all live and production sound, lighting, and tape for weekly worship celebrations and education needs.
- Power-user on a variety of software programs; know processes and means to create desired media outcomes for video and graphic applications; for more intense software programs such as video compositing and 3-D rendering this requires a continuous learning curve.
- Coach and develop assistants in specific technical areas for purpose of content creation.
- Know setup and operation for laptop and desktop computers for presentation use, including configuration into video systems.
- Location video operation: Operate broadcast cameras and related field equipment, including field lighting, battery maintenance and optimization, field audio for video, and recording deck(s).
- Various off-line video editing functions, including logging all footage, refining script, picking shots, using time code from logs.
- Various on-line video editing functions, including digitizing all footage, creating graphics in video compositing software, importing music, compiling all together in video editing system, "sweetening" audio, creating effects.
- Must know how to set up and operate basic sound and lighting configurations; must know technical specifications for how amplified sound works and how to troubleshoot potential problem areas.
- Decision maker on issues regarding the technical management of video, sound, lighting, and tape duplication.
- Troubleshooting on all video and computer graphic production and presentation equipment.
- In-house expert for anything technical!

and further duties as needed or assigned . . .

Copyright

Probably the most confusing and rumor-laden aspect of media in church life surrounds the issue of copyright. Truly, the issues are straightforward as they apply to worship and educational settings within the context of the church community.

The basic applicable legal code is buried under Section 110 of the Copyright Law of 1976 (17 U.S.C. §110[3]). Section 110 states that, without fear of breaking the law, churches may

1. perform non-dramatic literary or musical works and religious dramatic and musical works.
2. display individual works of a non-sequential nature (17 U.S.C. §101) during services at a house of worship or other religious assembly.

"Display," as defined in legalese, means to "show a copy of [a work] either directly or by means of a film, slide, television image, or any other device or process or, in the case of a motion picture or other audiovisual work, to show individual images nonsequentially."

Translated into common English, this means churches may

1. perform contemporary songs, regardless of the owner/copyright holder.
2. show any still image, regardless of its source, and even show frames of a film, if they are not in sequence during worship. This includes scanned images of any sort, including newspaper headlines, periodicals, pictorial books, or whatever you dream up.

What churches may NOT do during worship, according to Section 110(3):

1. Show any (pre-copywritten) motion picture, video or audio-visual work in its entirety or by segment, as this is neither a non-dramatic nor musical work, nor is it "displayed" (according to the non-sequential definition above).

2. Record programs from broadcast television, then show in worship, as this involves both the illegal duplication of a copywritten work, and the display of sequential images.

3. Play any non-live performed recording of a musical work, for example from CD or cassette tape.

4. Reproduce lyrics in any fashion from a copyright-protected musical work, including display of lyrics within projected graphic images and printing of the lyrics in bulletins and other forms.

Further, Section 110(1) makes the same applications for media use in non-profit educational environments.

Outside of worship and the classroom, things get much grayer. This includes posting of works on the Internet, and sale of works to other churches or individuals. Much is made of the exemption in the copyright law for fair use. When contemplating if something may be qualified as fair use, keep the following guidelines in mind:

- The more creative a work, the less likely it is to be covered by the fair use clause.

- Although no specific percentages apply, the more of a work that is used, the less chance it is covered by fair use.

- The impact of usage on a work's market value; the more it decreases its value, the less likely it is to be fair use.

 As a rule, never use fair use in a blanket way.

The only activities covered in a blanket way by fair use, according to standard intepretations of the First Amendment, are news reporting, research, and criticism. Anything else should be determined on a work-by-work basis.

This even applies to parody, one aspect of the fair use clause. Instances in which parody may suffice as a defense of potential audio-visual copyright violation might include the use of pre-recorded music with original dramatists, as in a skit or video version of a skit or TV show. However, be sure to check with a copyright lawyer on a case-by-case basis.

Fortunately, licenses exist for churches to circumvent the inability to show motion pictures and display song lyrics, two staples of a church that uses electronic media. These include:

- Motion Picture Licensing Corporation, P.O. Box 66970, Los Angeles, CA 90066. (800) 462-8855. The MPLC offers an umbrella license for a number of studios available for a small yearly fee (not more than $95) to cover films already available for rental.

- Swank Motion Pictures, 201 S. Jefferson Avenue, St. Louis, MO 63103-2579. (800) 876-5577, www.swank.com/comprevid.html. Swank offers copies with license for public showings of films not yet available for rental.

- Criterion Pictures, 800-890-9494.

- CCLI, OR Christian Copyright Licensing International, 17201 N.E. Sacramento, Portland, OR 97230. 800-234-2446.

For further information, consult *A Copyright Primer for Educational and Industrial Media Producers, 2nd Edition*, by Esther S. Sinofsky, and a local copyright lawyer.

Pre-Event Checklist
❏ Power

❏ 1. Power to all units, including those with safety features necessitating individual power-up?

❏ 2. Communication system powered on and all belt pack units plugged in?

❏ Computer System

❏ 3. Graphics file(s) copied from removable drives or network drives onto computer's internal hard drive?

❏ 4. Graphics file(s) finalized with all relevant song lyrics, scripture references, message points, copyright references, and checked for spelling?

❏ 5. Changes made after technical rehearsal?

❏ 6. All other applications closed to free RAM?

❏ Cameras

❏ 7. Power source established, with backup batteries, if needed?

❏ 8. Mounted and balanced on pedestals?

❏ 9. White balanced with appropriate light levels?

❏ 10. All appropriate video cables connected and secured?

❏ 11. Rear camera (studio) controls, if any, operational?

❏ 12. Signal established?

❏ 13. Checked in display(s) for image quality?

❏ Switcher/router(s)

❏ 14. All sources properly routed to mixing console?

❏ 15. Digital effects turned off and cleared, if any?

❏ 16. Audio faders down?

❏ Projector/Monitors

❏ 17. Powered?

❏ 18. Checked with color bars for image quality/consistency?

❏ 19. Consistent signal gain between cameras, computer, and video sources?

❏ 20. Edges of signal seamless with screen edges?

❏ And . . .

❏ 21. Scripts and other materials in place?

❏ 22. Videos in playback units and cued?

❏ 23. Tape for archiving/recording in deck and cued, with color bars/audio tone/header at front of tape?

❏ 24. All audio levels for recording set?

Director's Commands

Have you ever driven with cruise control? Going up a hill or around a curve with cruise can be an exhilarating and sometimes frightening experience, because the cruise setting has no concept of time. In fact, drivers using cruise for the first time are often amazed how often they unwittingly slow down their rate of speed when approaching a difficult section of highway.

A live production is much like driving with cruise control engaged. As much as we'd sometimes like, there is no way to stretch time to fit a complicated section of the event highway. When these moments happen, the only way to get through them without a massive wreck is to lead the production crew with a steady and calm voice, speaking a language that everyone understands.

Effective communication in this manner is paramount to a successful live production. Director's commands provide consistent language, regardless of the crewmember or the director. Commands internalized make for quick reaction time, which is helpful when the mistakes become twenty feet large!

Add black

To technical director, use video mixer fader to remove luminance from displayed video image, if available.

Add white

To technical director, use video mixer fader to add luminance to displayed video image, if available.

Advance Mac/PC

To computer operators, move to the next graphic image in the sequence of the event.

Center

To camera operators, compose the subject in frame using the rule of thirds.

Cut to

To crew, take previewed shot immediately without dissolves or effects.

Fade out/to black

To technical director, fade displayed image to black using video mixer.

Gain

To camera operators, adjust camera gain control to compensate for too much/too little luminance as directed.

Iris

To camera operators, adjust camera aperture to compensate for too much/too little light in frame as directed.

Pan

To camera operators, move frame left/right as directed.

Ready

To crew or individual operators, alert upcoming command/action.

Take

To technical director, perform standard cut or dissolve to previewed image.

Tilt

To camera operators, move camera up/down as directed.

Zoom

To camera operators, adjust focal length as directed.

Sample Script

A typewritten, columned script of the live event literally puts everyone involved on the same page, and removes any unnecessary interpretation. Effective scripts will make cues for when to display and when to quit displaying a particular graphic, video or live shot, in coordination with other communication forms of the live event, including spoken and read elements. An example of what a script might look like:

Source	Description	Subpoint	InCue	OutCue
PC	Graphic-Point 2	Waiting on God	"waiting"	
		Paul's trip		
CAM	Speaker	Persevere;	"persevere"	
		Set up clip		
VID	Video-"Rudy" clip	Perseverance	"little Rudy"	After clip
BLK	(wait for clapping)			
CAM	Speaker	God is faithful	"God"	

Glossary

A dictionary for the meta-langauge of electronic media production.

▶ Alpha channel

A computer generated keying channel for 2D and 3D graphics and video applications. A keying channel implies the "clear" part in which no signal or data exists, allowing the existing signal or data to be laid over another channel.

▶ Amplifier

An electronic device for increasing voltage and power of a video or audio signal. Types of devices include microphone preamps, mixing booster amps and distribution amplifiers.

▶ Anti-aliasing

Smoothing of aliasing effects by filtering and other techniques in computer applications. Aliasing is an effect generated when horizontal or diagonal lines in computer and video displays have noticeable "stair-stepping" or "jaggedies" by display resolution detail being too low.

▶ Aperture

See Iris

▶ Aspect ratio

The relationship of horizontal and vertical dimensions in image displays. Computer and video displays have an aspect ratio of 4:3; film has an aspect ratio of 16:9, which explains the technique of "letterboxing" or "pan and scan" that is necessary for film to be converted to video.

▶ Back focus

Adjustable portion of the lens on industrial and broadcast cameras that may determine the rear of the focal depth. See focal depth.

▶ Balanced

Circuitry that causes the audio signal to swing plus and minus of the system's ground reference. Noise induced into both wires of a cable run will cancel at the input of a balanced device.[1]

▶ BNC

A round, metal, locking cable connector found on composite, component, and Y-C video cables, as well as computer network cables.

▶ Character Generator (CG)

A computer system for providing electronically generated graphics and titles of various sizes and forms. Increasingly replaced by desktop computer systems.

▶ Chroma keying

A keying channel in which the range of signal, to be overlaid or dropped out, is defined by a specific color, usually blue or green. The color must be uniform throughout the keying range for successful overlay to occur. See alpha channel.

▶ Clearcom

A brand name for two-way headset communication systems used in live electronic media productions. Individual units consist of headsets, belt packs, and a cable, with one central base receiver for each chain.

▶ Clipping

A harsh form of audio distortion in which a signal's waveform is flattened by a system's inability to deliver any higher voltage.[2]

▶ Color bars

Video test signal consisting of a series of vertical bars of fully saturated color: white, yellow, cyan, green, magenta, red, blue, black. Used to adjust brightness, contrast, hue, and chrominance of monitors and projection systems.

▶ Color corrector

Circuitry that can pinpoint a small band of the color spectrum, with minimal effect on other colors in the spectrum. Will adjust the gain (amplification), black level, and gamma (tonal contrast) of the separate red, green, and blue channels in component video.

▶ Color temperature

The temperature of light affects its color. Although the human eye compensates for this phenomenon, a camera lens does not, which dictates the need for white balancing and color filters. Typically, daylight color temperature is ≥ 5500°K, and tungsten, or incandescent, light is 3200°K.

▶ Component video

A video signal in which luminance and chrominance are separated into three colors: red, green, and blue, with the addition of a separate sync pulse.

▶ Composite video

Video signal in which luminance, chrominance, and sync pulses are combined. Composite cable features BNC, or RCA, style connectors.

▶ Compression

The removal of data from a signal, used primarily in computer applications, in which bandwidth considerations must be taken into account. Typical compression schemes include JPEG, AIFF, Motion-JPEG, and MPEG 1 and 2. Compression removes like data based on user-defined keyframes, or snapshots taken of the signal. It works well on video signals that do not change their subject point often, such as "talking heads."

▶ Compressor/limiter

A device that reduces input gain on audio signals as that signal increases. Limiting is infinite compression, in which output levels remain the same regardless of the amount of gain given to an input signal. Most units may adjust the point at which audio signals become compressed or limited.[3]

▶ Control track

A linear track recorded onto videotape at frame frequency as a reference for the running speed of a videotape recorder and for the positioning of video tracks. The videotape equivalent to sprocket holes in the edges of film. Not used on computer-based media files.[4]

▶ Decibel

Measurement system for the loudness of an audio signal; expressed in dB. Decibels are measured exponentially, not incrementally; sustained exposure to 85db or greater may cause hearing damage.

▶ Digitize

The encoding process that translates an analog video signal into digital form (1s and 0s), for purpose of manipulating in the digital realm.

▶ Director

Leader of the live event crew; gives commands for operation.

▶ DV

Digital video (DV) is a new video format that records digital data onto traditional magnetic tape. Variants include DVCPro and DVCAM.

▶ DVD

Digital Video Disc, a video playback format utilizing the same laser technology that compact disks employ along with MPEG compression. An increasingly popular consumer format that is slated to replace VHS videotape.

▶ Filter wheel

Function on most industrial and broadcast field cameras that compensates for variation in Kelvin temperature. Typically, setting one is for indoor light, two for sunny days outdoors, and three for overcast days outdoors.

▶ FireWire

Data transmission technology developed by Apple Computer to transfer data from digital videotape to computer hard drives. Technically known as IEEE 1394.

▶ Focal depth

The distance within which a frame's subject is in focus. Varies depending on the distance of the subject from the camera, the focal length, and the aperture. The more open the iris is (smaller f/stop #), the more shallow the depth of focus.

▶ Focal length

The relative position of the zoom (wide or telephoto).

▶ Focus

The front ring of a camera's lens, used to bring objects into clarity.

▶ Frame

The entire rectangular area within the eye of the camera, or what the camera sees. Aesthetically used to describe the collection and composition of all objects within the visible area of the lens. Also 1/30th of a second in video, or the single set of two fields that compose a video image.

▶ Frequency

Expressed in Hz, the number of vibrations of a sound wave per second. The range of the human ear 20Hz to 20,000Hz is, considered the standard for audio production.

▶ Gain

Artifical supplementation of the luminosity of the video signal through the addition of decibels of video signal. Creates brighter images while forsaking quality.

▶ Gate

A device that turns on an audio path when a signal is present and turns it off when the signal is absent. User adjustable.[5]

▶ Generations

Number of times that an original analog video source has been copied, or duplicated, onto another source. Applies to digital video in the context of the application of multiple compression codes to a video file.

▶ Graphical User Interface (GUI)

Developed by Apple Computers in the early 1980s with the Macintosh platform and more recently employed by Microsoft Windows operating system software. The current standard for all media-related computer software applications.

▶ High–Definition Television (HDTV)

Original broadcast color television standards of 525-line picture resolution were fashioned largely by the need to provide systems compatible with then existing black and white services. Electronics technology has moved to the point in which an upgrade to these obsolete standards may be achievable through HDTV, which approximately doubles the current number of lines of resolution and changes the aspect ratio of television to 16:9. See NTSC.

▶ Hue

The predominant sensation of color; e.g., red, green, blue. The hue is an adjustable setting on most display units in electronic media, on a scale of red to green.

▶ Image enhancer

Apparatus that can enhance picture detail, increasing edge sharpness of vertical, and perhaps horizontal, edges. It cannot compensate, however, for poor resolution or soft focus, or create detail that does not exist.

▶ Iris

The ring of many camera lenses, which determines the amount of light given to the image the camera sees. The more open it is (smaller f/stop #), the more light is let into the camera.

▶ JPEG

Compression scheme for computer graphics; the standard for most Internet graphics uses. Motion JPEG is the standard for most non-linear video editing systems.

▶ Kelvin scale

Temperature measurement system used in video for determining the color of light. The higher the Kelvin color temperature, the hotter (more blue) the light is.

▶ Lens, camera

A precision optical system consisting of a number of individual components controlling iris, focus, and zoom. Must be protected from water, shocks, grit, moisture, heat, and the like.

▶ Linear

A sequential style of video editing in which video is copied from one analog source onto another. Results in generation loss and an inability to modify completed sequences.

▶ Lines of resolution

Standard NTSC television makes video by creating 525 horizontal lines thirty times every second (frames), through a method of interlacing in which every other line of a frame is drawn in one-sixtieth of a second.

▶ Luminance

The true measured brightness of a surface. For example, snow has high luminance, reflecting 93-97 percent of the light falling on it but black velvet has low luminance, reflecting approximately one percent of light falling on it.

▶ Macintosh

Computer operating system with unique graphical user interface, well suited for graphic and video applications.

▶ Macro zoom

Second zoom component in the lens system of most industrial and broadcast cameras; used for extreme close-ups.

▶ Medium

A communication form, including oral, print, or electronic, through which messages are sent and received. All communication occurs through a medium or media.

▶ Mixer

See switcher.

▶ Moore's Law

The dictum that computer memory and processing speed doubles every two years. This has basically held true since 1967, when Gordon Moore made this marketing prediction at Intel.

▶ MPEG

Data compression scheme for video, with many revisions. MPEG-2 is the standard for DVD and HDTV.

▶ Multi-camera

A type of video production using multiple cameras simultaneously by composing shots with instantaneous switching between camera shots. Usually limited to studio and live, event-oriented production.

▶ Multimedia

The buzzword that encapsulates the assimilation of the electronic culture of the past generation. Literally, multimedia is the combination of any number of single media forms, including visual imagery, sound, text and interactivity, or touch. Figuratively refers to the industry developed using CD-ROM and Internet technology.

▶ Neutral density filter

A camera filter used to compensate unusually bright sunlight to prevent an overexposed iris, which may affect focal length. A 1/8 filter, as found on many cameras, closes the iris down two stops.

▶ Noise

Spurious information interfering with a signal. New developments in technology continue to decrease the threshold at which noise is introduced.

▶ Noise reduction

Generally refers to a multiband gating device that attenuates an audio signal when it is below an established threshold.[6] Used to reduce hiss and pop in a signal to the point that desired frequencies become predominant.

▶ Non-linear

A non-sequential style of video editing, where it is possible to edit out of time. Enables greater flexibility than traditional linear editing and is ideal for time-sensitive short-form project post-production. Usually digital, without generational loss.

▶ National Television Systems Committee (NTSC)

A broadcast group that established the standards for broadcast television in North America at 525 lines of horizontal resolution. Concessions in quality were made at the time of the standard setting to accommodate existing black and white televisions. Now commonly known as "Never Twice Same Color."

▶ RGB

Acronym for red, green, and blue, the basic color scheme of television and computer displays.

▶ Router

A device through which multiple image sources may be sent to a single output, usually a switcher. Useful with smaller switchers having limited input sources.

▶ Rule of thirds

Method of determining proper frame composition in which a frame is divided into nine squares and the dividing points used as references.

▶ Saturation

The extent to which a color has been diluted with white. If a hue is pure and undiluted, it has 100 percent saturation. As it becomes diluted, its saturation falls (e.g., red, at 100 percent saturation, becomes pink at fifteen percent saturation).

▶ Scan doubler/quadrupler

Device that emulates high-definition television by literally doubling, or quadrupling, the number of horizontal lines in a standard NTSC signal. Good for filling the sometimes visible space between lines in large projection images.

▶ Signal-to-noise ratio

Abbreviated as S/N and expressed in decibels, the ratio of noise to pure signal information.

▶ Single camera

A style of video production dependent on editing, in which one camera creates all video. Used in many film and non-live video productions.

▶ Special effects generator

A unit for creating various wipe patterns, keying effects, mattes, etc. Often housed within a switcher.

▶ Switcher

Device receiving inputs from various sources. It may have the ability to apply effects. Used by the technical director.

▶ Sync pulse

Timing reference in video, which keeps frames moving steady at thirty frames/second. Prevents distortion or loss of video signal. Sync pulses are maintained separately in component video, but travel with video in composite signals.

▶ Talking head

Footage of a person creating voiceover track during a video segment. Excessive use is derided in the video production community.

▶ Technical director

Switcher operator. Takes commands from director.

▶ Time Base Corrector (TBC)

Circuitry used to insert accurate sync pulses when incoming sync pulses are lost or distorted. In other words, makes the video smooth when it otherwise would jerk or drop out, removing jitter on videotape playback and correcting color errors. A primary difference between amateur and professional video.

▶ Time code

A permanent record of time recorded onto magnetic (analog) videotape. Ideal for multi-source editing situations, as tapes become switchable without losing valuable frame accurate data references. This is unnecessary in the digital editing world.

▶ Unbalanced

Audio circuitry that connects one wire of the audio path to the system ground. Cables are highly susceptible to noise pickup; unbalanced cables provide no defense against this possibility.[7]

▶ VITC

A type of time code, Vertical Integral Time Code.

▶ White balance

Mechanism and/or action that instruct the camera about setting for white and/or black. All other color is then based from this point.

▶ Zoom

Device controlling focal length, or how far "into" a shot the camera sees.

> # See page 3 for CD–ROM installation instructions.

[1] "Audio as a Second Language," Roy W. Rising, *VideoSystems*, August 1996, p. 66.
[2] Ibid.
[3] Ibid.
[4] *The Digital Fact Book*, ninth ed., Bob Pank, ed. Quantel Limited: Newbury, England.
[5] Rising, p. 67.
[6] Ibid.
[7] Ibid.